SERMON IN A SENTENCE

St. Catherine of Siena

SERMON IN A SENTENCE

*A Treasury of Quotations
on the Spiritual Life*

FROM THE WRITINGS OF

St. Catherine of Siena

DOCTOR OF THE CHURCH

*Arranged according to the Virtues of
the Holy Rosary
and Other Spiritual Topics*

Selected and Arranged by
JOHN P. McCLERNON

IGNATIUS PRESS   SAN FRANCISCO

Cover art by Christopher J. Pelicano
Cover design by Roxanne Mei Lum

Frontispiece by Edith Beckwith Smith
Combermere, Ontario, Canada

ISBN 1-58617-020-1
Library of Congress Control Number 2003115831
Printed in the United States of America ∞

O sweet holy treasure of the virtues! You walk securely everywhere—on sea, on land, in the midst of enemies. You fear nothing, because God is hidden within you, God who is eternal security.

—St. Catherine of Siena

DEDICATION

This work is dedicated to my wonderful and supportive wife, Mary, and to the fruit of our marriage, the five beautiful children with whom God has blessed us: Christopher, Clare, Catherine, David, and Stephen.

A word of thanks and appreciation to my mother, Judy McClernon, who once again has provided sound advice and discernment in sorting through and selecting these "gems" from the writings of St. Catherine of Siena.

I also wish to thank the Dominican Order, which has nursed and mothered many a saint to holiness down through the ages. St. Catherine of Siena is a true daughter of St. Dominic, who founded this great order in order to learn, promote, and defend the fullness of truth in the Catholic Church. She is the patroness and spiritual mother to the Third Order Dominicans, which has been such a blessing to Mary and me in our walk with the Lord, and in our marriage and family life. I will always be in debt to the Dominicans. It gives me great pleasure finally to be able to give something back in the form of this little book of wisdom from the pen of the Seraphic Virgin.

Last, but certainly not least, I wish to thank St. Catherine of Siena for the treasure house of spiritual wealth she has left the Catholic Church and world through her famous *Dialogue*, along with her letters and recorded prayers. One can easily sense the fire of her total love for Christ and His Church. St. Catherine of Siena is really the author of this book. It is a privilege to be an instrument in bringing her advice and teachings to souls.

CONTENTS

Foreword   11
Introduction   13
Acknowledgments   15
Abbreviations   19
St. Catherine of Siena   21

ROSARY VIRTUES

The Joyful Mysteries
1. The Annunciation of Our Lord: *Humility*   33
2. The Visitation to Elizabeth: *Love of Neighbor* 39
3. The Birth of Jesus: *Spirit of Poverty*   46
4. The Presentation in the Temple: *Obedience*   52
5. The Finding of the Child Jesus in the Temple:
   Piety   60

The Sorrowful Mysteries
1. The Agony of Jesus in the Garden: *Sorrow
   for Sin*   69
2. The Scourging at the Pillar: *Purity*   76
3. The Crowning with Thorns: *Courage*   83
4. The Carrying of the Cross: *Patience*   90
5. The Crucifixion: *Self-Denial*   97

The Glorious Mysteries
1. The Resurrection of Jesus from the Dead:
   Faith   105
2. The Ascension of Jesus into Heaven: *Hope*   112
3. The Descent of the Holy Spirit: *Love of God*   119

4. The Assumption of Mary into Heaven:
    Desire for Heaven   127
5. The Crowning of Mary Queen of Heaven
    and Earth: *Devotion to Mary*   134

                    OTHER TOPICS
Prayer   143
The Eucharist   149
Confession   155
The Church   158
The Papacy   165
The Priesthood   169
Marriage and Family Life   176
The Mass   178
Baptism   180
The Bible   183
The Saints   185

FOREWORD

The motto of the Dominican Order is "Truth". In her Dominican environment, St. Catherine was driven to know truth and to live it in her daily life, even from childhood. In her boundless charity, especially for the Church, she labored endlessly to encourage others to do likewise.

To know the truth is to know things as they are. To live the truth is to be what one had been designed to be, by the wise and fatherly Creator.

Although St. Catherine was intensely involved in both human and divine spheres of activity, her dedication to truth enabled her to be at one with herself, with God, and with neighbor. Revealed truth and natural truth cannot be in conflict with one another, for truth cannot be in conflict with itself.

It is in this framework of truth that Catherine's words are best understood and applied to one's own life. The introduction of God's words into her own learning, living, and preaching, especially through her *Dialogue*, follows the pattern of her life—gathering and disseminating truth, for the purpose of living it.

In applying her lessons to our own lives we are helped, as she was, by the virtues of faith, hope, and charity. Through faith, our pursuit of truth sees God as the

Ultimate Truth, the measure of what we know and of what we are. Through charity, we are united with that Truth in a personal, mutual bonding of wills, called friendship. Through hope, we have, with clear confidence, the expectation of maturing that friendship, begun in Baptism, and enduring throughout eternity.

Other elements of the supernatural life of grace are seen in her supreme commitment to justice, one of the four moral virtues, especially in her practice of religion, her mutual relationship with God. Among the seven gifts of the Holy Spirit, wisdom, piety, and fortitude are featured prominently in her own life and in her ministry to others.

In the midst of a hectic and often frustrating life, St. Catherine found quiet and restoration in the "little cell" of her internal resources by engaging in conversation with God and with His "holy ones" who had traveled the road before her. It is for such moments in our lives that John McClernon has gathered into this little treasury the words of an excellent teacher and motivator, God's enthusiastic instrument of Truth, St. Catherine of Siena and, through her, the inspiration of our God.

Father Edward Robinson, O.P.
Dominican Priory of St. Albert the Great
Irving, Texas
January 2004

INTRODUCTION

There are many Catholics who would like nothing better than to read the actual writings of the Church's spiritual giants. But how many do? All too often the time needed to feed the soul takes a back seat, and one ends up spiritually starved. *Sermon in a Sentence* is designed for just such a person.

Imagine spending a few minutes with St. Catherine of Siena, a Doctor of the Church and certainly one of the more influential mystics in the history of Christianity. This famed Dominican saint has been called "the Seraphic Virgin" in part for the beauty and remarkable insights of her writings, most notably her spiritual classic *The Dialogue*. St. Catherine's knowledge and practical teachings on the spiritual life and union with God have inspired many a saint, for her advice and wisdom draw a soul like a magnet directly to the heart of God. This book has been designed to bring the inspiration of her words to you in a very simple and direct format.

Hundreds of quotations and short sayings taken from the writings of St. Catherine of Siena have been classified by the Christian virtues of which they speak and then arranged to complement the classic fifteen-decade Rosary, proceeding from the first joyful mystery (the Annunciation, with its virtue of humility) to the fifth glorious mystery (the Crowning of Mary, with its virtue of devotion to Mary). For those who choose to use these excerpts for meditation while reciting the Rosary, we have placed a type ornament after the tenth one, to mark the end of a decade. Additional quotations follow, for use with a Rosary or for separate meditation. A selection of quotations on other spiritual topics of interest follows, bringing the reader a sample of St. Catherine's reflections on such subjects as prayer, the Eucharist, the Church, and family life.

It is hoped that this little book will serve as an effective introduction to one of our great spiritual masters. May these quotes and short sayings find a place in your heart and soul and draw you closer to our Lord Jesus Christ, Whom St. Catherine loved and served so well.

ACKNOWLEDGMENTS

The author gratefully acknowledges permissions granted (if necessary) to reprint excerpts from the following sources:

The Dialogue of the Seraphic Virgin Catherine of Siena. Translated from the original Italian by Algar Thorald. Rockford, Ill.: TAN Books and Publishers, 1974. Originally published in 1906 by Kegan Paul, Trench, Trubner and Co. London. Text used was digitized and the English modernized by Harry Plantiga, Director of Christian Classics Ethereal Library ("CCEL") at www.ccel.org. Further modifications by John McClernon. Page references are cited from the TAN Books edition, a reprint of an edition published in 1959 by Newman Press, Westminster, Md.

Catherine of Siena: The Dialogue. Translation and introduction by Suzanne Noffke, O.P. The Classics of Western Spirituality. New York: Paulist Press, 1980. Copyright 1980 by Paulist Press, Inc. New York/Mahwah, N.J. Used with permission of Paulist Press at www.paulistpress.com.

The Letters of St. Catherine of Siena, vol. 1. Translated by Suzanne Noffke, O.P., vol. 202. Medieval and Renaissance Texts and Studies. Tempe, Ariz.: Arizona State University, 2000. Copyright 2000 by the Arizona Board of Regents for Arizona State University.

The Voice of the Saints: Counsels from the Saints to Bring Comfort and Guidance in Daily Living. Selected and arranged by Francis W. Johnston. Rockford, Ill.: TAN Books and Publishers, 1986. First published in 1965 by Burns and Oates, London. Copyright 1965, Burns, Oates, and Washburne. Reprinted with the permission of the Continuum International Publishing Group.

Saint Catherine of Siena, by Alice Curtayne. Rockford, Ill.: TAN Books and Publishers, 1980. First published in 1929 by Sheed and Ward, Ltd., London. Copyright renewed in 1980 by Alice Curtayne.

The Adoring Rosary with St. Catherine of Siena, by the Dominican Nuns of the Monastery of Our Lady of the Rosary, Summit, N.J. Citations reprinted by permission of Paulist Press from *Catherine of Siena: The Dialogue.* Translation and introduction by Suzanne Noffke, O.P. New York: Paulist Press, 1980. Copyright 1980 by Paulist Press, Inc., New York/Mahwah, N.J. Used with permission of Paulist Press at www.paulistpress.com.

The Prayers of Catherine of Siena. Translated and edited by Suzanne Noffke, O.P. Second edition. Lincoln, Neb.; San Jose, Calif.: Author's Choice Press, 2001. Copyright 2001 by Suzanne Noffke.

Scripture quotations have been taken from the following editions of the Holy Bible:

The Holy Bible, containing the Old and New Testaments. Revised Standard Version. Catholic Edition. Old

ABBREVIATIONS

A   *The Adoring Rosary with St. Catherine of Siena*, by
        the Dominican Nuns of the Monastery of Our
        Lady of the Rosary. Summit, N.J. Citations
        reprinted by permission of Paulist Press from
        Catherine of Siena: The Dialogue. New York: Paulist
        Press, 1980.

C   *Saint Catherine of Siena*, by Alice Curtayne.
        Rockford, Ill.: TAN Books and Publishers,
        1980.

D1   *The Dialogue of the Seraphic Virgin Catherine of
        Siena*. Translated from the original Italian by
        Algar Thorold. Rockford, Ill.: TAN Books and
        Publishers, 1974.

D2   *Catherine of Siena: The Dialogue*. Translated by
        Suzanne Noffke, O.P. New York: Paulist Press,
        1980.

L   *The Letters of St. Catherine of Siena*. Vol. 1. By St.
        Catherine of Siena. Translated by Suzanne
        Noffke, O.P. Tempe, Ariz.: Medieval and Renais-
        sance Texts and Studies, 2000.

P   *The Prayers of Catherine of Siena*. Translated and
        edited by Suzanne Noffke, O.P. Lincoln, Neb.:
        Author's Choice Press, 2001.

V   *The Voice of the Saints: Counsels from the Saints to Bring Comfort and Guidance in Daily Living.* Rockford, Ill.: TAN Books and Publishers, 1986.

St. Catherine of Siena

(1347–1380)

Doctor of the Church

Virgin and Patroness of Italy

Truly one of the more brilliant and influential women saints in the history of Christianity is St. Catherine of Siena. Catherine Benincasa lived only thirty-three years, but her brief adult life was filled with relentless apostolic activity, culminating in her offering her life for the unity and honor of the Holy Catholic Church and for the papacy she so strongly defended and upheld. It was a fitting death for this incredible woman, who so tirelessly labored, taking all measures, material and spiritual, to restore and uphold peace in the Church. She was in all ways a true spiritual daughter of St. Dominic, and she has rightly been called the great "social mystic", exemplifying the balance of contemplation and action that is a hallmark of Dominican spirituality. St. Catherine certainly ranks among the great mystics and spiritual writers of the Catholic Church, and she was an inspiration and model for many of the saints who lived later. One of the great women in the history of Western Europe, she was instrumental in renewing, restoring, and furthering the Christian ideal in her world. Over six hundred years later, she remains one of the more popular and loved saints.

In the year 1347 Catherine was born in Siena, Italy, on the feast of the Annunciation. She and her twin sister, who died not long after birth, were the youngest children of Lapa and Jacomo Benincasa, a prosperous wool dyer, whose bustling household included married couples and grandchildren as well as his own large family. From an early age some saints evidence special graces from God, and Catherine was certainly one of these. There are many pious childhood legends of Catherine, who at a young age was receiving the visions and mystical experiences that would mark her entire life. Notable among these was her vision of our Lord over the Dominican church in Siena, a vision that may well have indicated her later vocation. Catherine saw Jesus sitting on a throne and dressed in papal garments, surrounded by Ss. Peter, Paul, and John the Evangelist. The Lord smiled at Catherine and blessed her with the sign of the cross. Six years old at the time of this vision, Catherine developed a love for prayer and solitude, advanced in virtue, and displayed spiritual wisdom well beyond her years. She exhibited to her family and neighbors a pleasant, vibrant, and outgoing personality. The Benincasa family's pet name for the merry girl was "Euphrosyne", which is Greek for "Joy" and is also the name of an early Christian saint.

Catherine continued to have visions of Christ, Mary, various saints, and angels. At the age of seven the young girl had already privately vowed herself to the service of God as a virgin. Catherine also embraced the penitential life, as evidenced by her severe penances and prolonged fasts. By the time she had reached the age of eleven Catherine refused to eat meat, and a year later she resisted all efforts by her family to arrange a well-connected marriage for her. Lapa Benincasa tried in vain to enhance her pretty daughter's features and graceful figure in order for her to attract a good husband. Catherine would have none of this, and her response to her mother's efforts was to cut her long, golden brown hair in protest. Her furious mother promptly dismissed all the household servants and set Catherine to do all the work of running the large Benincasa household. She gave her no private time or place for her prayers. True to form, the pious girl lovingly and without complaint served her family and efficiently carried out all of the household chores. Jesus appeared to Catherine at this trying time in her life, and He urged her simply to "turn inward to the cell of your own soul, and there will be both a time and a place to find Me always." He taught her to look upon her service to the family as though she were serving His mother and the apostles, and thus she was able to meet this challenge with grace.

One day her father happened upon Catherine while she was on her knees deep in prayer and saw a white dove hovering over her head. Puzzled yet eventually convinced of their daughter's vocation, her parents decided to give Catherine the freedom to live as she felt called. A small, dimly lit room was set apart for her private use, and it was here that she gave herself to even more prayer and fasting. At seventeen, after a dream in which St. Dominic beckoned her, Catherine took on the habit of a Third Order Dominican. The tertiaries of that time followed an approved rule of life in the spirit of St. Dominic, wore a Dominican habit, but remained living at home.

The next three years Catherine increased her personal asceticism, eating and sleeping very little and leaving her home only for the nearby Dominican church, where she attended daily Mass and sought the spiritual direction of the friars. She enjoyed an almost continual sense of the presence of Christ, interspersed with violent temptations from the devil. At times Catherine endured long periods of feeling completely abandoned by God, and she once prayed, "O Lord, where were You when my heart was so sorely vexed with foul and hateful temptations?" She heard a voice saying, "Daughter, I was in your heart, fortifying you by grace." This time in her life culminated when, in her twentieth year, Catherine was given the rare grace of a "mystical espousal" to the Lord. While praying in her room, Jesus Christ, accompanied by His mother and many of the heavenly hosts, appeared to Catherine. The Blessed Mother took her hand and held it up to Christ, as He placed a ring on Catherine's finger and espoused her to Himself. (This ring would be visible only to Catherine the rest of her life as a reminder of the abiding presence of Jesus.) "Be of good courage", He told her; "you are now armed with a faith that will overcome all temptations." Catherine soon was made aware that she was to go and serve Him by serving her family and her neighbors.

There was no turning back for Catherine, who from this point forward embraced an all-consuming, active ministry of service to God, His Church, and His people. Like other Dominican tertiaries, she gave herself to the service of the poor and sick—distributing alms, visiting and converting prisoners, and volunteering in a Siena hospital. It was here that Catherine managed to make the most difficult patients fond of her, and she cared for those no one else would go near, notably those suffering with leprosy or advanced cancer.

Catherine's abundant supernatural gifts and holy life attracted many followers. These disciples became known as the "Caterinati". Many of Catherine's early letters were written to one of her disciples. She affectionately referred to them as her "spiritual family", "children" given to her by God that she might help them along the way of perfection. It was reported that Catherine was able to read their thoughts and frequently knew their temptations. Prominent among those Catherine influenced were her two Dominican confessors, other priests and religious, the famed artist Vanni (who painted her portrait), the poet Neri de Landoccio dei Pagliaresi, and an English hermit named William Flete, who left his hermitage to be near Catherine. He said, "I find greater peace of mind and progress in virtue by following her than I ever found in my cell."

Public opinion at this time in Siena and the surrounding towns and villages was sharply divided over what might be the driving force behind this young and energetic woman. Many people considered Catherine a saint, while others denounced her as a fanatic or hypocrite and even drummed up false charges against her. She was eventually summoned to Florence to appear before a general Chapter of Dominicans, where all these charges were disproved. Not long after this, Raymond of Capua was sent by the Dominicans to Siena in order to be the lector at the Dominican church there. He also was appointed to be Catherine's confessor and spiritual director, and thus began the pious association of these two future saints. Himself destined to be one of the great fourteenth-century Dominicans, Blessed Raymond of Capua became one of Catherine's champions and disciples, and after her death he was one of her first biographers. He was later elected Master General of the Dominican Order, which he helped to revitalize.

When Catherine returned to Siena from Florence, she found the city devastated with the plague, which would tragically take the life of up to one-third of the local population. She and her band of followers worked night and day to relieve the many plague sufferers. A priest who knew Catherine from childhood later noted, "Never did she appear more admirable than at this time. She was always with the plague-stricken: she prepared them for death; she buried them with her own hands. I myself witnessed the joy with which she nursed them and the wonderful efficacy of her words, which brought about many conversions." Some, including Blessed Raymond of Capua, were miraculously healed of this deadly disease because of her prayers.

Although called by God to a very active apostolate, Catherine's whole life was very much rooted in prayer. Blessed Raymond remarked, "As soon as she was freed from the occupations in which she was engaged for the work of souls, at once, one might say almost by a natural process, her mind was raised to the things of heaven."

By 1370 she gave up eating altogether and subsisted the last ten years of her life on the Eucharist alone. She received the stigmata in 1375 while praying in front of a crucifix in a church in Pisa. She fainted from the pain and the wounds remained, although they were invisible to all but Catherine until her death, when others could see the stigmata on her body. Catherine delivered many from diabolical possessions, performed many miracles, frequently levitated during prayer, and was graced with a very intimate relationship with Jesus and the Blessed Mother.

The fourteenth century was a time of great chaos and social unrest in Italy and within the Church. Class conflicts, revolutions, and family feuds were common in the Italian city-states, some of which were staunch anti-papal associations. Because of Catherine's growing reputation for holiness and miracles, she was asked to arbitrate many of these disputes. Her more than four hundred letters to European kings, princes, churchmen, and political leaders reveal a prolific letterwriting career. She was quite successful at settling differences, healing old feuds, and restoring many rebellious Italian cities to obedience to the Holy See. By the sheer force of her personality many were converted to Christ. Some of the most hardened sinners repented at the mere sight of her. Her gifts of healing were so powerful that at one time three Dominican priests were assigned to hear the confessions of those she convinced to repent and receive the Sacrament of Penance.

Catherine saw that there were three main wounds afflicting the Church in her day: the corruption of many of the clergy, the disunity of Christian Europe, and the absence of the popes from Rome. Regarding the papacy, history best knows Catherine for convincing Pope Gregory XI to return to Rome, thus ending seventy-five years of papal residence in Avignon, France. In an effort to unite feuding princes around a noble cause, Catherine had been a firm supporter of this Pope's campaign for another crusade to free the Holy Sepulchre from the Turks, and this eventually led to her correspondence with Gregory himself. He was ready to return to Rome, but had been largely deterred by the French cardinals. Catherine strongly encouraged Gregory to return, telling him, "My soul, which is united with God, burns with thirst for your salvation, for the reformation of the Church, and the happiness of the whole world. But it seems to me that God reveals no other remedy than peace." In 1376 Catherine finally met Pope Gregory face to face in the papal palace in Avignon. She boldly exclaimed, "Fulfill what you have promised", reminding him of a vow he had once taken with God and had never disclosed to anyone. Gregory considered this infused knowledge as a supernatural sign from God, and he acted upon it at once, returning to Rome early in 1377.

When she returned to Siena, Catherine dictated to her secretaries while in ecstacy what has become known as *The Dialogue*, a book that gives an account of her conversations with God the Father about various spiritual topics and concerns, such as the way of spiritual perfection, obedience, prayer, and Divine Providence, as well as other matters of importance to the Church and society of her time. Blessed Raymond of Capua was to remark, "She occupied herself actively in the composition of a book which she dictated under the inspiration of the Holy Ghost." This was her crowning work, and it has rightly been regarded as one of the great spiritual classics and inspirational works of all time. In it she repeatedly refers to God as "First Gentle Truth", who is the "Essence of Charity"—a God in love with mankind. A dominant theme throughout *The Dialogue* is the portrayal of the Son of God, Jesus Christ, as the sure way of Truth—a Bridge provided by God the Father between heaven and earth. "His doctrine is true", God the Father says to Catherine, "and has remained like a lifeboat to draw the soul out of the tempestuous sea to conduct her to the port of salvation. . . . He is the Way, the Truth, and the Life.

That is, the Bridge which leads you to the height of Heaven."

Catherine embodied the Dominican ideal of embracing the Truth with a passionate love. A Truth that is not only to be understood and accepted, but to be guarded and defended at all costs. She clearly saw the Catholic Church as the mystical Body of Christ on the earth. It is evident that Catherine was driven to employ every possible means to restore peace in the Church.

Catherine suffered constantly due to her own austerities, to her stigmata, and because of the state of the Church. After the death of Gregory XI in 1378 and the election of Urban VI to replace him, the "Great Schism" ensued when dissident French cardinals tried to elect their own pope. This schism tore at the heart and soul of the fourteenth-century Church, and Catherine's heart and soul were spiritually torn as well. Christendom was divided, and Catherine wore herself out trying to bring about reconciliation and unity. Many a letter was dispatched to the prelates, princes, and leaders of Europe, including Urban VI, warning him to control his harsh and arrogant temper. Urban accepted her advice and summoned Catherine to Rome so that he might profit by her prayers and counsel. The respect and admiration she had achieved in the eyes of many church and secular leaders is nothing short of remarkable for a woman of her time. On many occasions—at Siena, Avignon, Rome, and other European cities—learned theologians and scholars had questioned her and been humbled by the wisdom of her replies.

Although only thirty-three, her life was soon to be over. Burdened with sorrow over the terrible schism, she offered herself as a victim to God for the Pope and

Church unity. Her final prayer was "Lord, you are calling me to come to you, and I am coming to you—not
with any merits of my own but only with your mercy. I
am begging you for this mercy in virtue of your Son's
most sweet blood. . . . Father, into your hands I surrender my soul and my spirit." She died in Rome on
April 29, 1380. Not long after her death the imminent
riots and uprisings in Rome came to an end.

St. Catherine's body was found to be incorrupt in 1430.
She was canonized in 1461 by Pope Pius II, and in 1939
St. Catherine and St. Francis of Assisi were declared
co-patron saints of Italy. Pope Paul VI in 1970 declared
Catherine of Siena and Teresa of Avila the first women
Doctors of the Church.

> "O eternal Trinity, you are a bottomless ocean. The more
> I throw myself into the ocean, the more I find you, and
> the more I find you, the more will I search. I can never
> say of you, it is enough. . . . I have seen and tasted your
> bottomless depths, O eternal Trinity, the beauty of all
> that is created."
> —St. Catherine of Siena

THE
JOYFUL
MYSTERIES

The First Joyful Mystery

The Annunciation of Our Lord

Humility

Whoever humbles himself like this child, he is the greatest in the kingdom of heaven.—Matthew 18:4

[GOD:] This is the way, if you will arrive at a perfect knowledge and enjoyment of Me, the Eternal Truth, that you should never go outside the knowledge of yourself.
(D1 32)

[GOD:] By humbling yourself in the valley of humility, you will know Me and yourself, from which knowledge you will draw all that is necessary. (D1 32)

[GOD:] Charity, it is true, has many offshoots, like a tree with many branches. But what gives life to both the tree and its branches is its root, so long as that root is planted in the soil of humility. (D2 40)

[GOD:] The soul escapes dangers by her true humility, and by her prudence, flies all the nets of the world.
(D1 60)

[GOD:] One does not arrive at virtue except through knowledge of self and knowledge of Me, which knowledge is more perfectly acquired in the time of temptation, because then man knows himself to be nothing, being unable to lift off himself the pains and vexations which he would flee. (D1 119)

[GOD:] While man lives is his time for mercy, but when he is dead comes the time of justice. He ought, then, to arise from servile fear and arrive at love and holy fear of Me. Otherwise there is no remedy against his falling back. (D1 141)

[GOD:] Every perfection and every virtue proceeds from charity, and charity is nourished by humility. (D1 151)

[GOD:] I want them, in time of conflict, to take refuge in me by seeking me and knowing me as their benefactor, in true humility seeking me alone. This is why I give them these troubles. And though I may take away their comfort, I do not take away grace. (D2 113)

[GOD:] I withdraw Myself from the soul by sentiment, that she may be thus led to enclose herself in the house of self-knowledge, where is acquired every perfection. (D1 156)

[GOD:] The pride of the Devil cannot resist the humble mind, nor can any confusion of spirit be greater than the broadness of My good mercy, if the soul will only truly hope therein. (D1 162–63)

❦

[GOD:] Knowledge of self requires [perseverance] to be seasoned with knowledge of Me, lest it bring the soul to confusion. (D1 167–68)

[GOD:] By love you are made, and had My love been drawn back, that is, had I not loved your being, you could not be, but My love created you. (D1 178)

[GOD:] I tell you . . . it is far better to walk by the spiritual counsel of a humble and unschooled person with a holy and upright conscience than by that of a well-read but proud scholar with great knowledge. (D2 157)

[GOD:] Even when [my servants] see something that is clearly sinful they do not pass judgment, but rather feel a holy and genuine compassion, praying for the sinner and saying with perfect humility, "Today it is your turn; tomorrow it will be mine unless divine grace holds me up." (D2 190)

[GOD:] The soul who lives virtuously places the root of her tree in the valley of true humility. (D1 200)

[GOD:] Know yourselves and the instability of the world. (D1 209)

[GOD:] Without Me you can do nothing. (D1 227)

[GOD:] His labor may be reputed to be in vain, who watches the city if it be not guarded by Me. All his labor will be vain if he thinks by his labor or solicitude to keep it, because I alone keep it. (D1 251)

[GOD:] The just man does not turn his head to admire his past virtues, because he neither can nor will hope in his own virtues, but only in the Blood in which he has found mercy. (D1 260)

[GOD:] A soul is obedient in proportion to her humility, and humble in proportion to her obedience. This humility is the foster-mother and nurse of charity, and with the same milk she feeds the virtue of obedience. (D1 284)

[GOD:] Many have appeared to be perfect who have afterwards turned back. (D1 295)

[GOD:] Never leave the cell of self-knowledge, but in this cell preserve and spend the treasure which I have given you, which is a doctrine of truth founded upon the living stone, sweet Christ Jesus. (D1 329–30)

[GOD:] There, [in souls] where pride is, can be no obedience.... [A] man's humility is in proportion to his obedience, and his obedience to his humility. (D1 299)

[C:] I am she who is not. . . . You alone are He who is. And my being and every further grace that You have bestowed upon me I have from You, who give them to me through love, and not as my due. (D1 275)

[C:] You are infinite, and we are finite. (D1 276)

[C:] Don't be proud—it will coarsen your understanding. (C 47)

[C:] Self-knowledge is the dwelling in which we discover our own lowliness, and this makes us humble. (L 145)

[C:] And since pride blinds us, impoverishes us, and dries us up by robbing us of the richness of grace, it leaves us unfit to govern ourselves or anyone else. (L 167)

[C:] In recognizing that we are nothing we humble ourselves. And in humbling ourselves we enter that flaming, consumed heart, opened up like a window without shutters, never to be closed. (L 8)

[C:] Let everything you do be done in fear and love of God. Remember that one day you must die, and you do not know when. God's eye is upon you and watches over all you do. (L 28)

[C:] We certainly are sparks! This is why you want us to humble ourselves. Just as sparks receive their being from the fire, so let us acknowledge that our being comes from our first source. (L 43)

[C:] What you have to do, do with humility. For the devil is cast out not by the devil but by the virtues of patience and humility. (L 58)

[C:] Once we see that of ourselves we are nothing at all, we are completely humbled at the knowledge of what our benefactor has done for us. We so grow in love when we recognize God's great goodness at work in us. (L 115)

[C:] [W]ithin the heart of Christ crucified, consumed and opened up for us ... your soul will be filled and fattened with virtue, and suddenly you will discover these two wings, humility and charity, that will allow you to fly to eternal life. (L 225)

The Second Joyful Mystery

The Visitation to Elizabeth

Love of Neighbor

You shall love your neighbor as yourself.
—Mark 12:31

[GOD:] Whatever you do in word or deed for the good of your neighbor is a real prayer. (D2 127)

[GOD:] If you do not love me you do not love your neighbors, nor will you help those you do not love. But it is yourself you harm most, because you deprive yourself of grace. (D2 33–34)

[GOD:] Very pleasing to Me, dearest daughter, is the willing desire to bear every pain and fatigue, even unto death, for the salvation of souls, for the more the soul endures, the more she shows that she loves Me. (D1 38)

[GOD:] Every virtue is obtained by means of your neighbor. (D1 39)

[God:] You will find yourself deprived of my mercy unless you turn to compassion and kindness. (D2 35)

[God:] You are all obliged to help one another by word and doctrine, and the example of good works, and in every other respect in which your neighbor may be seen to be in need; counseling him exactly as you would yourselves, without any passion of self-love. (D1 40–41)

[God:] Love of Me and of (your) neighbor are one and the same thing, and so far as the soul loves Me, she loves her neighbor, because love towards him issues from Me. This is the means which I have given you, that you may exercise and prove your virtue. (D1 45)

[God:] Inasmuch as you can do Me no profit, you should do it to your neighbor. This proves that you possess Me by grace in your soul, producing much fruit for your neighbor and making prayers to Me, seeking with sweet and amorous desire My honor and the salvation of souls.
(D1 45)

[God:] I could easily have created men possessed of all that they should need both for body and soul, but I wish that one should have need of the other, and that they should be My ministers to administer the graces and the gifts that they have received from Me. (D1 47)

[God:] [Love] your neighbor without being loved by him and without consideration of your own advantage, whether spiritual or temporal, but loving him solely for the praise and glory of My Name, because he has been loved by Me. (D1 194–95)

[GOD:] In charity for their neighbors they find me. (D2 131)

[GOD:] Not only is virtue proved in those who render good for evil, but many times a good man gives back fiery coals of love, which dispel the hatred and rancor of heart of the angry, and so from hatred often comes benevolence. (D1 49)

[GOD:] I take delight in few words and many works. (D1 55)

[GOD:] Perfect virtue cannot exist and give fruit except by means of the neighbor. (D1 60)

[GOD:] Discern my will rather than ... judge other people's intentions. (D2 195)

[GOD:] I give My servants hunger and desire for My honor and the salvation of souls. (D1 72)

[GOD:] If a man carry away the vessel which he has filled at the fountain and then drink of it, the vessel becomes empty, but if he keeps his vessel standing in the fountain while he drinks, it always remains full. So the love of the neighbor, whether spiritual or temporal, should be drunk in Me. (Di 155)

[God:] You cannot repay the love which I require of you, and I have placed you in the midst of your fellows, that you may do to them that which you cannot do to Me. (Di 155)

[God:] Love your neighbor of free grace, without expecting any return from him, and what you do to him I count as done to Me. (Di 155–56)

[God:] There cannot be love of Me without love of the neighbor, nor love of the neighbor without love of Me. (Di 170)

[God:] It is necessary to bear with others and practice continually love to one's neighbor, together with true knowledge of oneself. (Di 193)

[God:] If you should see evident sins or defects, draw out of those thorns the rose, that is to say, offer them to Me with holy compassion. (Di 219)

[God:] Apparent sinners may frequently have a good intention, for no one can judge the secrets of the heart of man. That which you do not see you should not judge in your mind. (Di 219)

[GOD:] Because the soul remains always in the love of her neighbor, she remains always in Mine, and thus remains united to Me. (D1 220)

[GOD:] I am their Judge, not you. (D1 220)

[C:] The habit of judging keeps the soul far from Thee, so I do not wish to fall into this snare. (D1 205–6)

[C:] I would rather go without a cloak than without charity. (C 31)

[C:] Even if you should often find yourself surrounded by opposition, don't let that deter you from giving others your best efforts for God's honor. This, I see, is the way the holy disciples acted. (L 51)

[C:] Now, while we have time—and the time is ours—let's give our neighbors our best efforts, and God our praise. (L 256)

[C:] Let your souls rise up like people in love and reach out to love what God loves most, our dear sisters and brothers. Rise up with such longing and conceive such a great love that you would gladly give your lives to restore them to the life of grace and save them. (L 297)

[C:] We are divided from one another in hatred and bitterness when we ought to be bound by ties of blazing divine charity—a bond so strong that it held the God-Man nailed fast to the wood of the most holy cross. (L 137)

[C:] We cannot say that we have nothing to give him. No, we should take the wine of his indescribably thirsty desire for our salvation, and give it back to him in the person of our neighbor. (L 142)

[C:] The more you love God, the more your love will reach out to your neighbors, helping them spiritually and materially as you have opportunity and time to serve them. Thus will God's will be fulfilled in us, which wants nothing other than that we be made holy. (L 193)

[C:] Divisions originate only from seeing others' faults while failing to see our own, and from not knowing how or being willing to put up with each other's faults. Let's not be that way. No, bind yourselves together in the bond of charity, loving and supporting one another. (L 225)

[C:] Hatred of our neighbors is nothing less than an offense against God. So we ought to hate more the fact that we hate, since First Truth is offended by it. . . . Those who live in mortal hatred are in fact hating themselves more than their enemies. (L 286)

[C:] When you free your soul from hatred you make peace with God and you make peace with your neighbors. (L 287)

[C:] Let us ask for mercy, and God will grant it. Let us not be concerned about judging our neighbors or taking vengeance on them. For it behooves me to give to others the mercy I want for myself.   (L 289)

THE THIRD JOYFUL MYSTERY

THE BIRTH OF JESUS

Spirit of Poverty

Blessed are the poor in spirit, for theirs is the kingdom of heaven.
—Matthew 5:3

[GOD:] Without me they could never be satisfied even if they possessed the whole world. For created things are less than the human person. They were made for you, not you for them, and so they can never satisfy you. Only I can satisfy you. (D2 98)

[GOD:] They do not see except with blind eyes, since their desire is fixed on passing things, and so they are deceived and act like fools who notice only the gold and fail to see its venomous sting. (D2 95)

[GOD:] The goods of the world, all its delights and pleasures, if they are got and had apart from me with selfish and disordered love, are just like scorpions. (D2 96)

[GOD:] The affection, stripped of self-love, mounts above itself and above transitory things. (D1 138)

[GOD:] Though they may possess the riches of the world, they must own them humbly, not with pride, as things lent to them rather than as their own—for in my generosity I give you these things for your use. (D2 96)

[GOD:] The righteous man is able to endure privation. (D1 175)

[GOD:] You have as much as I give you: you keep as much as I allow you to keep; and I give and let you keep as much as I see would be good for you. This is the spirt in which people should use things. (D2 96)

[GOD:] Those . . . who live miserably in the world [make] a god of created things and of their own sensuality, from which comes damage to their body and soul. (D1 199)

[GOD:] All consolations are thorns that pierce the soul who loves them disordinately. (D1 141)

[GOD:] The earth is unable to satisfy. . . . I alone can satisfy [you]. (D1 203)

❧

[GOD:] They owe their first love to me. Everything else they should love and possess . . . not as if they owned it but as something lent them. (D2 97)

[GOD:] Man is placed above all creatures, and not beneath them, and he cannot be satisfied or content except in something greater than himself. Greater than himself there is nothing but Myself, the Eternal God. Therefore I alone can satisfy him. (D1 203)

[GOD:] Know the transitory nature of things of the world, all of which pass like the wind. But this you cannot know thoroughly, unless you first recognize your own fragility. (D1 208)

[GOD:] Everything was theirs only on loan, and . . . as debtors they have to give an accounting to me. (D2 267)

[GOD:] You must take the key in your hand and walk by the doctrine of My Word, and not remain seated, that is to say, placing your love in finite things, as do foolish men. (D1 286)

[GOD:] I provide for the poor, and for their poverty they will be given the greatest of riches. (D2 312)

[GOD:] Look at God made man, clothed in the lowliness of your humanity. (D2 320)

[GOD:] So the rich are left sad while my poor are happy. . . . Because they leave everything they possess me completely. The Holy Spirit becomes the nurse of their souls and their little bodies in every situation. (D2 323)

[God:] With this faith and hope, ablaze with the fire of charity, my true servants leaped and leap above riches and selfishness. Just so, the glorious apostle Matthew leaped up from his tax booth and, leaving his great wealth behind, followed my Truth. (D2 319)

[C:] In the earth we can recognize our own poverty: we see that we are not. For we *are* not. We see that our being is from God. (L 8)

[C:] Oh, Supreme and Eternal Truth, I am the thief and You have been punished for me. For I see Your Word, Your Son, fastened and nailed to the Cross, of which You have made me a Bridge. (D1 76–77)

[C:]Though [deluded people] seek honors they are disgraced; in pursuit of riches they are poor, because they are not looking for genuine wealth; wanting happiness and pleasure they find sadness and bitterness, because they lose God, who is supreme happiness. (L 14)

[C:] [Do] not let yourself be deluded by human weakness or by the leprosy of greed; for neither possessions nor anything or anyone else will answer for you, but only courageous virtue and a good conscience. (L 36)

[C:] [Prefer] those true solid virtues that appear small and insignificant in the eyes of the world, but that hold within themselves the treasure of grace. (L 128)

[C:] The foolish pleasures of the world pass and come to naught.... [You] cannot hold on to them, cannot keep life or health or any created thing from passing away like the wind. (L 132)

[C:] We have the most satisfying, most gratifying, most mighty lordship there is—lordship over the city of our own soul. (L 133)

[C:] There are many who have been victorious over a city or a fortress, but if they have failed to conquer themselves and their enemies—the world, the flesh, and the devil—one could say they have nothing at all. (L 134)

[C:] We ought to be more willing to lose temporal things and bodily life than spiritual goods and the life of grace. The former are finite, but God's grace is infinite. It brings us infinite good, and so the loss of it is an infinite evil. (L 136)

[C:] Let no one then, nor any status or grandeur, any power or other human glory (all of which are empty and vanish like the wind) lure us away from this true love, our soul's life and glory and happiness. (L 148)

[C:] God didn't free you from the world for you to be immersed and drowned in the world through attachment and inordinate desire. Have you then more than one soul? No. For if you had two, you could give one to God and the other to the world. (L 178)

[C:] Don't be concerned about nobility or wealth, because virtue is the only thing that makes one noble, and the wealth of this world is the direst poverty when it is possessed apart from God with inordinate love. (L 178–79)

[C:] Don't rest your confidence in your physical youth or worldly power. A person is alive today, dead tomorrow; well today, sick tomorrow; a lord today, tomorrow a servant. How foolish then are people who are unduly attached to these things! (L 187)

[C:] It is an awesome thing to see the good gentle Jesus, the one who rules and feeds the whole universe, in such great want and need that no one else has ever been as poor as he. He is so poor that Mary hasn't a blanket to wrap him in. In the end he dies naked on the cross so that he might reclothe us and cover our nakedness. (L 206)

[C:] Use the things of this world as nature needs them, but without excessive attachment. For it would be very displeasing to God if you were to set your heart on something of less value than yourself. That would be nothing but a surrender of your dignity. For people become like what they love. (L 206)

[C:] Take a look at your soul and at how short time is; consider the fact that you must die, and you don't know when. (L 213)

[C:] The only reason you are wanting for material things is your abandonment of concern for the spiritual. (L 247)

The Fourth Joyful Mystery

The Presentation in the Temple

Obedience

If you love me, you will keep my commandments.
— John 14:15

[God:] The soul can, by her free will, make a choice either of good or evil, according as it pleases her will; and so great is this liberty that man has, and so strong has this liberty been made by virtue of this glorious Blood, that no demon or creature can constrain him to one smallest fault without his free consent. (D1 69–70)

[God:] The sign that you have this virtue [obedience] is patience, and impatience is the sign that you do not have it. (D2 327)

[God:] He is a Road in the form of the Bridge. And He says that He is the Truth, and so He is, because He is united with Me who am the Truth. And he who follows Him walks in the Truth and in Life. (D1 82)

52

[GOD:] It is not enough, in order that you should have life, that My Son should have made you this Bridge, unless you walk thereon. (D1 76)

[GOD:] It is the will that gives trouble to man. (D1 125)

[GOD:] Those who follow this road are the sons of the Truth, because they follow the Truth, and pass through the door of Truth and find themselves united to Me, who am the Door and the Road and at the same time Infinite Peace. (D1 82)

[GOD:] He practiced this doctrine and made the road by His actions, giving you His doctrine by example rather than by words; for He practiced, first Himself, what He afterwards taught you. (D1 86)

[GOD:] [You] become like what you serve. (D2 76)

[GOD:] My servants . . . desire nothing but what I desire. (D1 127)

[GOD:] The soul is free, liberated from sin by the Blood of My Son, and she cannot be dominated unless she consent with her will, which is controlled by her free choice. (D1 132)

[GOD:] You know that the commandments of the Law are completely contained in two, and if these two are

not observed the Law is not observed. The two commandments are to love Me above everything, and your
neighbor as yourself; [these] two are the beginning, the
middle and the end of the Law. (D1 137)

[GOD:] It is ... impossible to fulfill the law given by
Me, the Eternal God, without fulfilling that of your
neighbor, for these two laws are the feet of your affection by which the precepts and counsels are observed.
(D1 195)

[GOD:] Your desire [is] infinite.... I, who am the Infinite God, wish to be served by you with infinite service,
and the only infinite thing you possess is the affection
and desire of your souls. (D1 198)

[GOD:] Behold I have made you the road and opened
the door with My Blood. Do not then be negligent to
follow, laying yourselves down to rest in self-love and
ignorance of the road, presuming to choose to serve Me
in your own way instead of the way which I have made
straight for you by means of My Truth. (D1 214–15)

[GOD:] Rise up then, promptly, and follow Him, for
no one can reach Me, the Father, if not by Him; He is
the Way and the Door by which you must enter into
Me, the Sea Pacific. (D1 215)

[GOD:] I am joyful, and I keep the soul who clothes
herself in my will in supreme joy. I am that supreme

providence who never betrays my servants' hope in me in soul or body. (D2 290)

[God:] What caused the great obedience of the Word? The love which He had for My honor and your salvation. Whence proceeded this love? From the clear vision with which His soul saw the divine essence and the eternal Trinity, thus always looking on Me, the eternal God.
(D1 283)

[God:] Disobedience comes from pride, which issues from self-love, depriving the soul of humility. The sister given by self-love to disobedience is impatience, and pride, her foster-mother, feeds her with the darkness of infidelity. (D1 284–85)

[God:] The whole of your faith is founded upon obedience, for by it you prove your fidelity. (D1 285)

[God:] [Be obedient] to my holy commandments in the mystic body of holy Church. (D2 176)

[God:] Oh! blessed obedience! You voyage without fatigue, and reach without danger the port of salvation, you are conformed to My only-begotten Son, the Word, you board the ship of the holy cross ... so as not to transgress the obedience of the Word, nor abandon His doctrine. (D1 289)

[God:] You have been commanded to love Me above everything, and your neighbor as yourself. No gloss has been put upon these words as if it should have been said, if your neighbor injures you do not love him; but they are to be taken naturally and simply, as they were said to you by My Truth, who Himself literally observed this rule. (D1 292)

[God:] Take ... the key of obedience with the light of faith, walk no longer in such darkness or cold, but observe obedience in the fire of love, so that you may taste eternal life. (D1 292)

[God:] The great key of general obedience ... opens the door of Heaven. (D1 303)

[God:] The perfectly obedient man rises above himself and his own sensuality. (D1 305)

[God:] The road of true obedience ... is a road of truth founded by the obedient Lamb, My only-begotten Son. (D1 316)

[God:] Everything that the obedient man does is a source of merit to him. (D1 323–24)

[God:] The obedient man speaks words of peace all his life, and at his death receives that which was promised him . . . that is to say, eternal life, the vision of peace and of supreme and eternal tranquility and rest. (D1 325)

[GOD:] Obedience nourishes both body and soul in peace and quiet. (D1 319)

[GOD:] Like good shepherds, [follow] the Good Shepherd, My Truth, whom I gave you to lead your sheep, having willed that He should give His life for you. (D1 245)

[GOD:] If you ask Me where obedience is to be found, and what is the cause of its loss, and the sign of its possession, I reply that you will find it in its completeness in the sweet and amorous Word, My only-begotten Son. (D1 281)

[GOD:] I have appointed you all to labor in the vineyard of obedience in different ways. (D1 320)

[C:] I always put the will of God before that of men. (C 124)

[C:] Faithful obedience would have wrought more in the sight of God and in the hearts of men than all your human prudence. (C 174)

[C:] I beg you to fulfill my longing to see you united with and transformed in God. But this is impossible unless we are one with his will. (L 7)

[C:] Be obedient, then, for love of that most gentle loving young Man, God's Son, who obeyed even to the
point of death. (L 52–53)

[C:] I want you to want things to go not your own way
but the way of the one who is. You will then be stripped
of your own will and clothed in his. . . . Let's accept every
circumstance with reverence. (L 51)

[C:] He wanted to be an obedient servant, not a vio-
lator of the law or of his Father's will. He always sought
his Father's honor and our salvation. So let's follow in
his footsteps. (L 61)

[C:] The temptations and wiles of the devils, the flesh,
and the world may come shooting poisoned arrows. . . .
But unless lady freedom consents to these disordered sug-
gestions, she never sins, because sin is in the will alone.
(L 151)

[C:] No one can refuse to keep these sweet holy
commandments—not on the grounds of nobility or
wealth or power or success or greatness. None of us can
deny that we are servants. These commandments were
given us by gentle First Truth, who was our rule and
our way. (L 192)

[C:] By his obedience he gave us grace again. So I beg
you tenderly in Christ Jesus: let's follow this way and
rule of the true holy commandments, . . . remembering

the blood of God's Son so that we may be the more inspired to keep them. Oh how sweet is this servitude that frees us from the servitude of sin! (L 192)

[C:] God in his infinite goodness has given us the light of knowledge, by which we recognize that virtue, serving our Creator, gives us life. (L 240)

[C:] May God give you grace to choose the best course in this, and make all you do serve his honor and the good of your soul. (L 9)

THE FIFTH JOYFUL MYSTERY

THE FINDING OF THE CHILD JESUS
IN THE TEMPLE

Piety

You . . . must be perfect, as your heavenly Father is perfect.
—Matthew 5:48

[GOD:] I am not a respecter of persons or status but of holy desires. In whatever situation people may be, let their will be good and holy, and they will be pleasing to me. (D2 97)

[GOD:] As soon as you are filled with my love and love of your neighbor, you will find yourself in the company of the multitude of solid virtues. Then the soul's appetite is ready to be thirsty—thirsty for virtue and my honor and the salvation of souls. (D2 108)

[GOD:] If these souls do not abandon the exercise of holy prayer and their other good works, but go on, with perseverance, to increase their virtues, they will arrive at the state of filial love. (D1 145)

[GOD:] I desire nothing but [the soul's] sanctification, which is certified to her in the Blood of My Son. (D1 154)

[GOD:] [A man filled with my love] follows on with anxious desire, thirsting after the way of Truth, in which way he finds the Fountain of the Water of Life, through his thirst for My honor and his own salvation and that of his neighbor. (D1 138–39)

[GOD:] In the beginning a man serves Me imperfectly through servile fear, but, by exercise and perseverance, he arrives at the love of delight, finding his own delight and profit in Me. This is a necessary stage, by which he must pass, who would attain to perfect love, to the love that is of friend and son. (D1 150–51)

[GOD:] Where can [love for Me and for neighbor] be acquired? In the house of self-knowledge with holy prayer, where imperfections are lost, even as Peter and the disciples, while they remained in watching and prayer, lost their imperfection and acquired perfection. By what means is this acquired? By perseverance seasoned with the most holy faith. (D1 161)

[GOD:] The more the soul tries to loosen her affection from herself, and fasten it in Me with the light of the intellect, the more she knows, and the more she knows, the more she loves, and, loving much, she tastes much.
(D1 165)

[GOD:] How glorious is that soul who has indeed been able to pass from the stormy ocean to Me, the Sea Pacific, and in that Sea, which is Myself, the Supreme and Eternal Deity, to fill the pitcher of her heart. (D1 192)

[GOD:] In whatever state a man may be, he should never stop doing good. (D1 201)

[GOD:] The soul is never so perfect in this life that she cannot attain to a higher perfection of love. . . . Be ever ready to grow in greater perfection. (D1 196)

[GOD:] Every state of life is pleasing and acceptable to me if it is held to with a good and holy will. For all things are good and perfect, since they were made by me, and I am supreme Goodness. (D2 110)

[GOD:] I love virtue and hate vice. (D1 209)

[GOD:] As long as you are pilgrims in this life you are capable of growth, and he who does not go forward, by that very fact, is turning back. (D1 210)

[GOD:] If the soul truly has light, she will wish to arrive at perfection. (D1 210)

[GOD:] They may be called perfect who have abandoned the general way of living of the world. (D1 210–11)

[GOD:] It is true that the soul becomes more or less lighted according to the material which it brings to the fire; for although you all have one and the same material, in that you are all created to My image and [likeness,] and, being Christians, possess the light of holy baptism, each of you may grow in love and virtue by the help of My grace, as may please you. (D1 232)

[GOD:] You increase your strength in love, and your free-will, by using it while you have time, for when time is past you can no longer do so. (D1 232)

[GOD:] It is true that I desire you to use your being, and exercise the graces which I have bestowed upon you, in virtue using the free-will which I have given you. (D1 251)

[GOD:] Though I created you without your help I will not save you without it. (D1 251)

[GOD:] The conversations of a truly obedient man are good and perfect, whether they be with just men or with sinners, through his rightly ordered love and the breadth of his charity. (D1 308)

[GOD:] There is no sadness in charity, but the joy of it makes the heart large and generous. (D1 313)

[GOD:] With that very same measure with which a man measures to Me, does he receive in himself the measure of My goodness. Labor, therefore, to increase the fire of your desire. (D1 38)

[God:] Nothing is as easy and delightful as love. And what I ask of you is nothing other than love and affection for me and for your neighbors. This can be done any time, any place, and in any state of life by loving and keeping all things for the praise and glory of my name. (D2 110)

[God:] The love of virtue . . . marks my servants. (D2 173)

[God:] I am He who takes delight in few words and many deeds. (D1 204)

[God:] The soul is filled with love, seeing herself so much loved. (D1 78)

[God:] The Memory, the Intellect, and the Will . . . when these three powers are harmoniously joined together in My Name, all the other operations which the man performs, whether in deed or thought, are pleasing, and joined together by the effect of love, because love is lifted on high, following the Sorrowful Crucified One. (D1 79–80)

[God:] If the heart and the powers of the soul are drawn to Him, all the actions are also drawn to Him. (D1 80)

[God:] The soul is nourished in the life of grace. (D1 130)

[C:] Have no other wish than to be conformed with Christ crucified, always following in his steps, ablaze with love for virtue. (L 14)

[C:] Do what you have to do with joy and with a loving heart. (L 19)

[C:] It is a very consoling thing to live well and virtuously. (L 25)

[C:] Don't be thankless and unappreciative, because this could easily dry up the fountain of piety within. (L 39)

[C:] Sow, sow God's word! Make good on the talents entrusted to you! God has given you, and your neighbors as well, not merely one talent, but ten. These are the ten commandments, the very life of our soul. So be enterprising in your use of them. (L 43–44)

[C:] We are the ones for whom his blood was given as ransom. When we remember that ... every ill-ordered pleasure and hankering is scorned, and we are left clothed only in genuine solid virtue. (L 77)

[C:] If you seek only God's honor and other people's salvation, ... everything else you do will be done reasonably and justly. (L 100)

[C:] If you put your holy resolution into action, you will find Christians very willing to follow you. (L 149)

[C:] I long for you to be a productive field and to bear fruit, receiving the seed of God's word for yourself and for others. . . . We should [be] an example of virtue and decency. (L 176)

[C:] Let your heart and soul be set afire in Christ gentle Jesus, with love and longing to reciprocate such love, to give him life for life! He gave his life for you; decide now to give your life for him. (L 188)

[C:] When we are thus stripped of our every wish and clothed in God's will, we are very pleasing to God. Like an untethered horse we run swiftly from grace to grace, from virtue to virtue. (L 202)

[C:] Take hold of this lovely wedding garment of divine charity and put it on. This is how the soul dresses so as not to be thrown out from the wedding feast of everlasting life, to which God invited us and continues to invite us. (L 218)

[C:] The soul grounded in love accomplishes great things and does not avoid hard work. She . . . is constantly looking to how she can be united with the object of her love. Now this is how God's servants act. (L 224)

[C:] Is there anything better or more delightful than the task of building the edifice of our soul? How agreeable to have found the rock, the master architect, and the servant, the laborer needed for this building! Oh what a sweet architect is the eternal Father! (L 253)

THE
SORROWFUL
MYSTERIES

THE FIRST SORROWFUL MYSTERY

THE AGONY OF JESUS IN THE GARDEN

Sorrow for Sin

The cares of the world, and the delight in riches, and the desire for other things, enter in and choke the word, and it proves unfruitful.—Mark 4:19

[GOD:] Those who have felt heartfelt contrition, love for true patience, and true humility ... suffer with patience and so make atonement. (D2 29)

[GOD:] These souls have, then, a taste of eternal life ... they have let go of the hell of self-will. (D2 158)

[GOD:] Never, for any reason, must you sin. True charity knows this, for it always carries the lamp of holy discernment. (D2 44)

[GOD:] Neither the greatest of virtues nor any service to your neighbor may be bought at the price of sin.
(D2 44)

[GOD:] My sweetest daughter, your tears constrain Me, because they are joined with My love, and fall for love of Me. (D1 65)

[GOD:] My mercy is without any comparison, far more than you can see, because your sight is imperfect, and My mercy perfect and infinite. (D1 92)

[GOD:] [The sinner] is governed by that which is not, that is by sin, for sin in itself is nothing. (D1 93)

[GOD:] If they had repented in sorrow for having offended me and had put their trust in my mercy, they would have found mercy.... My mercy is incomparably greater than all the sins anyone could commit. (D2 268)

[GOD:] How great is the foolishness of men in making themselves feeble, when I have made them strong, and in putting themselves into the hands of the Devil. (D1 120)

[GOD:] The devil invites men to the water of death, that is, to that which he has, and blinding them with the pleasures and conditions of the world, he catches them with the hook of pleasure, under the pretense of good, because in no other way could he catch them. (D1 121–22)

[GOD:] The soul, from her nature, always relishes good, though it is true that the soul, blinded by self-love, does not know and discern what is true good, and of profit to the soul and to the body. (Di 122)

[GOD:] By sin . . . the world germinates thorns and tribulations, and because this river flows with tempestuous waters, I gave you the Bridge, so that you might not be drowned. (Di 124)

[GOD:] They that love me . . . drive away sin with contrition of the heart. (Di 127–28)

[GOD:] You know that every evil is founded in self-love, and that self-love is a cloud that takes away the light of reason, which reason holds in itself the light of faith, and one is not lost without the other. (Di 130)

[GOD:] Man, by his nature, cannot desire anything but good, and vice, appearing to him thus under the color of the soul's good, causes him to sin. But, because the eye, on account of its blindness, does not discern, and knows not the truth, it errs seeking good and delights there where they are not. (Di 131–32)

[GOD:] He who is wrapped in self-love is solitary. Why is he solitary? Because he is separated from My grace and the love of his neighbor, and being, by sin, deprived of Me, he turns to that which is naught, because I am He that is. (Di 136)

[GOD:] I do not wish the soul to consider her sins, either in general or in particular, without also remembering the Blood and the broadness of My mercy. (DI 162)

[GOD:] To be pleasing to Me you must enlarge your hearts and affections in My boundless mercy, with true humility. (DI 162)

[GOD:] One who despairs despises My mercy, making his sin to be greater than mercy and goodness. Wherefore, if a man fall into this sin, he does not repent, and does not truly grieve for his offense against Me as he should. (DI 267)

[GOD:] Do you think that sitting down and binding yourself with the chain of mortal sin, you can walk? or that without a key you can open the door? Do not imagine that you can. (DI 287)

[GOD:] Though it is true that they can obey the precepts of the law if they will, and have the time repenting of their disobedience, it is very hard for them to do so, on account of their long habit of sin. Therefore let no man trust to this, putting off his finding of the key of obedience to the moment of his death. (DI 290)

[GOD:] Although every one may and should hope as long as he has life, he should not put such trust in this hope as to delay repentance. (DI 290)

[C:] I will hide myself in the Wounds of Christ crucified, and bathe myself in His Blood and so shall my iniquities be consumed, and with desire will I rejoice in my Creator. (D1 163)

[C:] I know well that mercy is proper to you, so you cannot resist giving it to whoever asks you for it. (D2 275)

[C:] To sin is human, but to persist in sin is devilish. (V 73)

[C:] You may seem to yourself to be full of faults, but don't let that slow you down. God looks more to our good will than to our failings. (L 15)

[C:] Understand that the devil would like nothing better than to have you go over and over the knowledge of your wretchedness without anything else to season it. But that knowledge has to be seasoned with hope in God's mercy. (L 306)

[C:] I beg you, dearest brothers and sisters, to be reconciled and make peace with him, for he came to mediate peace between God and humanity. (L 25)

[C:] What a dangerous thing is sin in the soul! Of what great good it deprives us, ... it robs us of life. It takes away light, leaving darkness in its place. It strips away mastery in exchange for slavery. (L 61)

[C:] Now what would it be ... if we were masters of the whole world but not of the vices and sins within us? These rob us of the light of reason so that we cannot see how lost we are, nor how secure is the soul bound to the gentle Jesus. (L 61)

[C:] Oh what a terrible thing is sin, and how displeasing to God, since he did not let it pass unpunished but took out vengeance and justice for it on his own body! (L 116)

[C:] God wants us to be lovers of virtue and despisers of vice. Oh how sweet it will be for you to have this virtue! ... Sin is just the opposite: it leads one into every sort of misery. (L 116)

[C:] It was sin that killed our Father. Let us act as does a true son who sees his father's blood shed. A hatred grows within him for the enemy who has killed him. We act in the same way when we contemplate the blood of our Creator. (L 152)

[C:] We ought to take vengeance on ourselves—that is, on our evil thoughts, vices, and sins—because we ourselves are our own greatest enemy. (L 152–53)

[C:] Our sin has left us naked; we had lost the garment of grace. So Jesus gave up his own life and with it clothed us. (L 206)

[C:] Grace is a garment against which the devils have no power, because it strengthens and frees from every weakness. Sin is the only thing that weakens the soul. (L 218)

[C:] Awake and get up from the sleep of apathy. Learn from the gentle teacher of truth who gave his life as a true shepherd for those who will willingly heed his voice by keeping his commandments. (L 228)

[C:] Let fear of offending God always loom larger than any other suffering, and then you will never again have to be afraid. (L 243)

[C:] What kills sin and vice? Only hatred and love— the contempt I have conceived for sin, and the love I have conceived for virtue for God's sake. (L 261)

[C:] Up, then, courageously, while you are still in time, where it is possible to receive mercy! Run to Christ crucified, who will receive you kindly if only you are willing.
(L 278)

[C:] It seems he does not want to remember the offenses we commit against him; he does not want to condemn us for eternity but wants always to be merciful. So get up, my brother, if you want to be joined with Christ. (L 282)

The Second Sorrowful Mystery

The Scourging at the Pillar

Purity

Clean the inside of cup and dish first so that the outside may become clean as well.—Matthew 23:26

[GOD:] That inclination to sin, which remains from the original corruption, ... is indeed a source of weakness, but the soul can keep the bridle on it if she choose. Then the vessel of the soul is disposed to receive and increase in herself grace, more or less, according as it pleases her to dispose herself willingly with affection and desire, of loving and serving Me. (D1 69)

[GOD:] I call the soul "heaven" because I make heaven wherever I dwell by grace. I made the soul my hiding place and by my love turned her into a mansion. (D2 75)

[GOD:] Light is seen better near darkness, and darkness near light. (D1 115)

[GOD:] The virtues conceived, they give birth to themselves perfectly and imperfectly, according as the soul exercises perfection in herself. (D1 131)

[GOD:] [The soul] must advance to perfection ... by a generous love to Me with a pure and virtuous heart. (D1 144–45)

[GOD:] [Through self knowledge the soul is able] to root out the thorns of evil thoughts, replacing them with the stones of virtues. (D1 157)

[GOD:] They render praise and glory to My Name ... that they might participate in My beauty. (D1 176)

[GOD:] I created the soul to My own image and [likeness], placing her in such dignity and beauty. (D1 208)

[GOD:] [Love] Me in perfect purity, with no other regard than for the praise and glory of My Name, serving neither Me for her own delight, nor her neighbor for her own profit, but purely through love alone. (D1 215–16)

[GOD:] Unite yourself always to Me by the affection of love, for I am Supreme and Eternal Purity. I am that Fire which purifies the soul, and the closer the soul is to Me, the purer she becomes. (D1 218)

[GOD:] The further [the soul] is from Me, the more does her purity leave her, which is the reason why men of the world fall into such iniquities, for they are separated from Me. (D1 218)

[GOD:] You have greater dignity and excellence than the angels, for I took your human nature and not that of the angels. (D1 228)

[GOD:] In all souls I demand purity and charity, that they should love Me and their neighbor, helping him by the ministration of prayer. (D1 240)

[GOD:] [The just man has] bound sensuality like a slave with the rein of reason. (D1 259)

[GOD:] Do you think to be admitted to the marriage feast in foul and disordered garments? (D1 287)

[GOD:] Oh! fools and madmen, delay no longer to come out of the mud of impurity. (D1 291)

[GOD:] These are the true workers. They till their souls well, uprooting every selfish love, cultivating the soil of their love in me. They feed and tend the growth of the seed of grace that they received in holy baptism. (D2 62)

[GOD:] Free choice cuts itself off from sensuality and binds itself to reason. And then I dwell in their midst through grace. (D2 105)

[GOD:] You must exercise yourself in tearing out every perverse desire, whether spiritual or material. (D2 118)

[GOD:] I am supreme and eternal purity. I am the fire that purifies the soul. (D2 191)

[GOD:] The good shepherd washed the little sheep clean in his blood. (D2 245)

[GOD:] It is not enough for eternal life to sweep the house clean of deadly sin. One must fill it with virtue that is grounded in love. (D2 100)

[C:] With the Blood of this door—Your truth—have You washed our iniquities and destroyed the stain of Adam's sin. The Blood is ours, for You have made it our bath, wherefore You can not deny it to any one who truly asks for it. (D1 278–79)

[C:] As a man more readily sees spots on his face when he looks in a mirror, so the soul with true knowledge of self rises with desire and gazes with the eye of the intellect at herself in the sweet mirror of God, knows better the stains of her own face, by the purity which she sees in Him. (D1 62)

[C:] [Sinners] do harm to the world, being mirrors of sin when they ought to be mirrors of virtue. (D1 277)

[C:] If you make a holy resistance to temptations you will find in those thorns the fragrant rose of perfect purity.
(C 50)

[C:] I tell you, charity to our neighbors for God's sake is the fire that cleanses the soul. (L 15)

[C:] Come forth in the most perfect purity as iron comes out purified from the furnace. So I want you to shut yourself up in the open side of God's Son, that open storeroom so full of fragrance. (L 85)

[C:] Maintain bodily and spiritual purity. . . . Your effort will become a great delight and consolation to you. For just as vice is a source of spiritual sadness, so virtue always gives consolation and joy. (L 70–71)

[C:] Once our soul's jug is clean of sin and vice and filled with virtue, there is no holding the heart back or keeping it from loving. For it has discovered the spring of God's goodness at work in it, and is itself a reflection of its Creator, who created us in his own image and likeness. (L 124)

[C:] Let us follow in his footsteps, driving out vice by virtue: pride by humility, impatience by patience, injustice by justice, impurity by perfect chastity and continence. . . . Let a sweet holy war be waged against these vices! (L 152)

[C:] We ought constantly to fear offending so gentle and dear a Lord. This is a holy fear which like a servant enters quietly into our soul to cleanse us of every vice, of every sin, of every deed that might be contrary to our Lord's will. (L 127)

[C:] I want you to keep before yourself the memory of the blood of God's Son, shed with such fiery love. This will be for us a continual baptism of fire that will cleanse and warm our soul, relieving us of all the filth and chill of sin. (L 153)

[C:] You cannot dispense justice to others in good faith unless you are just with yourself, for what you do is only as just as your will is just and pure. (L 162)

[C:] Anyone who looks upon our Creator, the God-Man, slain on the wood of the most holy cross, will at once put a rein on every sensual and fleshly impulse. (L 185)

[C:] There is no tether to restrain us from running because we have cut ourselves loose from every disordered appetite and desire for our own will, which are the tethers and ties that keep the souls of spiritual persons from running free. (L 202)

[C:] Beware lest we be poisoned by selfish self-centeredness, by loving ourselves apart from God, giving our attention to the world's pleasures and prestige and making a god of our flesh. (L 187)

[C:] Once this weak body of ours and our sensual nature have been conquered, we will be the victors. Our reason, our soul, will be a free woman, in possession of God the supreme eternal Good. (L 189)

[C:] Ponder the fact that God has made you a gardener, to root out vice and plant virtue. (L 225)

[C:] He is a master architect who knows what we need, and he wants nothing else but that we be made holy. Whatever he gives and permits . . . he gives and permits it for our good, either to cleanse us of our sins or for our growth in perfection and grace. (L 253)

[C:] In remembrance of the blood is found the fire of blazing charity. . . . It burns and consumes whatever selfish love may exist in you, so that the fire of selfish fear and self-love is extinguished by the fire of this love. (L 304)

The Third Sorrowful Mystery

The Crowning with Thorns

Courage

Courage! It is I! Do not be afraid.—Matthew 14:27

[GOD:] If you have conceived the virtue of courage within you, you will always be strong and constant, and you will prove your courage externally through your neighbors. (D2 39)

[GOD:] Holy discretion is a prudence which cannot be cheated, a fortitude which cannot be beaten, a perseverance from end to end, stretching from Heaven to earth, that is, from knowledge of Me to knowledge of self, and from love of Me to love of others. (D1 59–60)

[GOD:] This power of Mine gives the virtue of fortitude to whoever follows this road, wisdom gives him light, so that, in this road, he may recognize the truth, and the Holy Spirit gives him love. (D1 87)

[GOD:] [It is My plan for My people] that they may conquer, proving their virtue, and receive from Me the glory of victory. (D1 118)

[God:] Courageously ... should the soul spur herself on with prayer as her mother. (D2 127)

[God:] No one should fear any battle or temptation of the Devil that may come to him, because I have made My [people] strong, and have given them strength of will, fortified in the Blood of My Son. (D1 118–19)

[God:] [The] soul having gathered together the two commandments, that is love of Me and of the neighbor, finds herself accompanied by Me, who am her strength and security, and walks safely because I am in the midst of her. (D1 138)

[God:] The soul always fears until she arrives at true love. (D1 151)

[God:] The soul, exercising herself in virtue, begins to lose her fear. (D1 189)

[God:] Participate in My strength and power, which strengthen the soul against her sensual self-love, against the Devil, and against the world. (D1 239)

[God:] [I] give supreme security to the soul who possesses Me through the affection of love. (D1 252)

[GOD:] Conscience always pulls in one direction, and sensuality in the other. But as soon as they decide courageously, despising themselves, and say, "I want to follow Christ crucified," . . . they discover my immeasurable tenderness. (D2 90)

[GOD:] Water grows solid under the feet of the obedient man. (D1 322)

[C:] Mount the donkey of our humanity and make it go only where reason may guide it. . . . I want you to do this with the greatest zeal, reciprocating the warmth of our King. This is the way to master our sensuality with a courageous heart. (L 18)

[C:] Zealously do what is in your power, giving honor to God and your best efforts to your neighbors, trusting that the Holy Spirit will do what seems impossible to you. (L 18–19)

[C:] Start being brave about everything, driving out darkness and spreading light as well. Don't look at your weakness, but realize that in Christ crucified you can do everything. (L 21)

[C:] I long to see you one of God's true knights, always following the path of virtue, never turning back to look at what you've plowed but keeping your eye on what you still have to do. . . . Never tire in doing what is holy and true. (L 35)

[C:] Follow the path of virtue as a courageous person would do. And don't dally, saying, "I'll do it tomorrow." For you aren't sure you'll have the time. It's just as our Savior said:"Don't be thinking about tomorrow. Sufficient for the day is its own concern." (L 36)

[C:] I assure you that supreme Goodness has prepared the times and the ways for us to do great deeds for him. This is why I told you to be eager to increase your holy desire, and not to be satisfied with little things, because God wants great things! (L 40)

[C:] Take up arms courageously so that no blow can pierce you. I am referring to the weapon of the most holy cross, which defends us against every blow and temptation from devils seen and unseen. If you keep [Christ's] blood in mind, you will be victorious. (L 57)

[C:] Give your lives for Christ. This is how you will prove yourself a true and courageous knight. (L 81)

[C:] Let's happily and joyfully, with flaming, blazing desire take up the true standard of the most holy cross, never fearing that we will not be able to persevere in the life we have begun. Let us rather say, "Through Christ crucified I will be able to do and endure all things." (L 77)

[C:] How blessed will be my soul and yours when you are standing on this battlefield, this stormy sea, armed with the weapon of charity! You will win this charity by keeping the cross in mind. (L 57)

[C:] Take courage, take courage and do not evade suffering. Always hold fast to a holy will that concentrates only on what Christ loved and on what he hated. When our will is thus armed . . . it will be granted such strength. (L 93)

[C:] If the devil should come with all sorts of illusions and different fantasies, and with slavish fear, trying to occupy our soul and mind, let us not be afraid, for all these things have become powerless because of the power of the cross. (L 93)

[C:] Take courage, . . . for when God engrafted himself into us barren trees by joining his divine nature with our humanity, he so strengthened our reason and our love for him that we are drawn to love by the power of love. (L 100)

[C:] Oh sweet holy treasure of the virtues! You walk securely everywhere—on sea, on land, in the midst of enemies. You fear nothing, because God is hidden within you, God who is eternal security. (L 129)

[C:] By his death he has given us life. By enduring insult and abuse he has restored our dignity. With his hands nailed fast to the cross he has freed us from the shackles of sin. . . . He has washed us with his overflowing blood. So we have nothing at all to fear. (L 134)

[C:] A man who knows he is well armed ought not be afraid. . . . See that God has equipped us with armor so strong that it cannot be pierced by the devil or anyone else. That armor is our free will. (L 150-51)

[C:] Let's not be afraid, because divine providence has out-fitted us so well that we have no reason for fear. Our armor is good, and our helper the best. For our helper is God, and he is such that no one can withstand him. (L 151)

[C:] As long as we continue to look to this strong lov-ing [God], we cannot be weakened by the thought of our own frailty. (L 151)

[C:] Once clothed and armored with virtue ... you will shed slavish fear and take possession of the city of your soul. You will never cringe before any possible blow of pain or difficulty, nor will you turn back. (L 187)

[C:] Let neither pleasure nor pain hold you back, but run along this road with courageous heart, finding your delight in virtue and in suffering for Christ crucified, who has so gently taught you how. (L 206)

[C:] Stay near your gentle mother, charity, who will free you from all fear and cowardice. She will give you courage and generosity and freedom of heart. She will make you strong, conformed to God, and she will make you one with him—for those who live in charity live in God. (L 231)

[C:] Everything will be accomplished in spite of what seems to us to be an obstacle. (L 262)

[C:] Courage, then! Let's persevere on our journey. Let's take heart, because in Christ crucified we can do everything! (L 260)

[C:] It is no longer time to sleep, because time does not sleep but is always passing like the wind. Raise up in yourself out of love the standard of the most holy cross. (C 80)

[C:] I do not see how any reform can be accomplished if you do not choose a number of holy men, who are virtuous and do not fear death. (C 144)

THE FOURTH SORROWFUL MYSTERY

THE CARRYING OF THE CROSS

Patience

As for [the seeds] in the good soil, they are those who, hearing the word, hold it fast in an honest and good heart, and bring forth fruit with patience.—Luke 8:15

[God:] Patience cannot be proved in any other way than by suffering, and patience is united with love. (D1 39)

[God:] You must all ... [seek] the glory and praise of my name through the salvation of souls, bearing up under pain and weariness, following in the footsteps of this gentle loving Word. There is no other way you can come to me. (D2 60)

[God:] If you will observe the virtues of fortitude and perseverance, these virtues are proved by the long endurance of the injuries and detractions of wicked men, who, whether by injuries or by flattery, constantly endeavor to turn a man aside from following the road and the doctrine of truth. (D1 49)

[God:] Patience ... proves that I am in the soul and the soul is in Me. (D1 54)

[God:] If virtue were not visible and did not shine in the time of trial, it would not have been truly conceived. (D1 60)

[God:] Patience [is] the queen who reigns over all the virtues because she is the heart of love. She is the sign and signal of the soul's virtues, showing whether or not they are rooted in me, eternal Truth. (D2 144)

[God:] No one born passes this life without pain, bodily or mental. Bodily pain My servants bear, but their minds are free, that is, they do not feel the weariness of the pain; for their will is accorded with Mine. (D1 125)

[God:] Time is no more than the point of a needle, and when time is over, so is suffering—so you see how small it is. Therefore . . . endure it patiently. (D2 93)

[God:] With perfect patience do they merit, and their labors are rewarded with infinite good. Hereafter they know that all labor in this life is small, on account of the shortness of time. (D1 128)

[God:] Love for her neighbors has made her patient. (D2 167)

[God:] If you desire to arrive at life you must persevere in virtue. . . . It is with perseverance that they who want life arrive at Me who am Life. (D1 134)

[GOD:] Persevere until you find Me, who am the Giver of the Water of Life, by means of this sweet and amorous Word, My only-begotten Son. And why did He say: "I am the Fountain of Living Water"? Because He was the Fountain which contained Me, the Giver of the Living Water. (D1 135)

[GOD:] You must have thirst, because only those who thirst are invited: "Whosoever thirsts, let him come to Me and drink." He who has no thirst will not persevere, for either fatigue causes him to stop, or pleasure. (D1 136)

[GOD:] I do not impose a heavier burden than the soul can bear, if only she is ready and willing to bear it for love of me. (D2 292)

[GOD:] How is a lively faith to be recognized? By perseverance in virtue. (D1 158)

[GOD:] [My servants] become mediators in prayer, in word, in good holy living, setting themselves up as an example to others. The precious stones of virtue shine in their patience as they bear others' sins. These are the hooks with which they catch souls. (D2 307)

[GOD:] [Patience] conquers and is never conquered. Her companions are courage and perseverance, and she returns home victorious. (D2 144)

[GOD:] The soul should advance by degrees. (D1 161)

[GOD:] Charity, the mother of patience, has given her as a sister to obedience, and so closely united them together that one cannot be lost without the other. Either you have them both or you have neither. (D1 283)

[GOD:] Who was more patient than He? for His cry was never heard in murmuring, but He patiently embraced His injuries like one enamored, fulfilling the obedience imposed on Him by Me, His Eternal Father. Wherefore in Him you will find obedience perfectly accomplished. (D1 284)

[GOD:] Oh! how sweet and glorious is this virtue, which contains all the rest, for she is conceived and born of charity, on her is founded the rock of holy faith. She is a queen whose consort will feel no trouble, but only peace and quiet; the waves of the stormy sea cannot hurt her, nor can any tempest reach the interior of the soul in whom she dwells. (D1 288)

[C:] Be impatient—with your miserable impatience. (C 47)

[C:] Have patience; and do not let your minds and hearts be filled with evil thoughts and fancies, which come from the devil to impede the honour of God and the salvation of souls and your own peace and quiet. (C 124)

[C:] But we, through enduring, shall win; because patience is never conquered, but is always the victor. (C 124–25)

[C:] Truth is silent when it is time to be silent, but when silent, it cries out with the cry of patience. (C 144)

[C:] Nothing great is ever done without much enduring. (C 148)

[C:] Do you know that you *pester* God with your great impatience? (C 47)

[C:] By humble and faithful prayer, the soul acquires, with time and perseverance, every virtue. (V 39)

[C:] I long to see you go forward like a brave knight, never turning back to escape the blows. Go constantly forward with true and perfect perseverance, for you know that it is not merely setting out but only perseverance that wins the crown. (L 24)

[C:] If persevering on this battlefield wearies you ... take up the holy standard of the cross. That sturdy pillar is the resting place of the Lamb slain for us. It is so strong that it relieves us of all weakness. (L 24)

[C:] I ... challenge you to a sweet and most holy patience, for without patience we cannot please God. I beg you then to take up this weaponry of patience so that you may receive the fruit of your troubles. (L 32)

[C:] Our gentle Savior crowns not those who begin in virtue but those who persevere in it. . . . He was the master of perseverance and the one who grants it. He did not give up in the face of our foolishness and ingratitude.

(L 70)

[C:] Persevere well and you will later receive the reward of supreme and eternal blessedness, where supreme eternal beauty resides. (L 71)

[C:] Since this holy cross is so sweet that it relieves all bitterness, pick it up for your journey along this road. For we pilgrim travelers need this holy wood for support until we have reached our destination, where our soul is at rest in our final home. (L 77)

[C:] Let us endure, let us endure, . . . no suffering will be so richly rewarded as weariness of heart and spiritual pain. These are the greatest sufferings there are, and so they are deserving of greater fruit. (L 93–94)

[C:] [Bear] trials with good, true patience. At that point we show our faith to be alive and not dead, in that we have conformed our will with God's. (L 120)

[C:] One is crowned and deserving of glory not for beginning but only for persevering. . . . How confounded that knight would deserve to be who turned and ran from the battlefield just as he was on the verge of winning!

(L 187)

[C:] [The soul] leaves behind the troubles and anxieties of the world and picks the fragrant rose of true holy patience, setting before her mind's eye the life-giving blood of the Lamb, set before us on this road. (L 209)

[C:] We must therefore bear this little trial willingly. Little, we may call it, like all our sorrows, because of the brevity of time; since no trial can last longer than our time in this life. How much time have we? It is like the point of a needle. (C 51)

THE FIFTH SORROWFUL MYSTERY

THE CRUCIFIXION

Self-Denial

If any man would come after me, let him deny himself and take up his cross daily and follow me.—Luke 9:23

[GOD:] These sufferings [which I set before you as a vessel] are found to be filled with the water of my grace, which gives life to your soul. (D2 46)

[GOD:] Works of penance performed alone without the . . . virtues would please Me little; often, indeed, if the soul perform not her penance with discretion, that is to say, if her affection is placed principally in the penance she has undertaken, her perfection will be impeded. (D1 50)

[GOD:] The more they have scorned pleasure and been willing to suffer, the more they have lost suffering and gained pleasure. Why? Because they are enflamed and on fire in my charity, where their own will is consumed.
(D2 146)

[GOD:] Souls . . . fail because of their fear of suffering.
(D2 114)

[GOD:] [Self-knowledge] is the knife which slays and cuts off all self-love founded in self-will. (D1 57)

[GOD:] I sent My Word, My own Son, clothed in your own very nature, the corrupted clay of Adam, in order that He might endure suffering in that self-same nature in which man had offended, suffering in His body even to the opprobrious death of the Cross. And so He satisfied My justice and My divine mercy. (D1 67–68)

[GOD:] Sufferings increase and strengthen virtue, make it grow and prove it. (D2 147)

[GOD:] This Bridge is lifted on high, and yet, at the same time, joined to the earth. Do you know when it was lifted on high? When My Son was lifted up on the wood of the most Holy Cross. (D1 78–79)

[GOD:] [The soul] finds her pleasure in feeding at the table of the most holy cross, that is, in patterning herself after the humble, patient, spotless Lamb, my only-begotten Son. (D2 163)

[GOD:] I had taken out [your] punishment on the body of my only-begotten Son. (D2 180)

❧

[GOD:] My gentle Truth . . . does not scorn any eager longing or labors offered to me. (D2 181)

[GOD:] I concealed My power in Him, letting Him suffer pain and torment like man, not that My divine nature was therefore separated from human nature, but I let Him suffer like man to satisfy for your guilt. (D1 107)

[GOD:] No one can pass through this life without a cross. (D1 124)

[GOD:] You have, then, two parts in you—sensuality and reason. Sensuality is appointed to be the servant, so that, with the instrument of the body, you may prove and exercise the virtues. (D1 132)

[GOD:] Souls ... were bought with Christ's blood. (D2 233)

[GOD:] He did not redeem you with gold or silver but with his blood in the greatness of his love. He did not redeem just half of the world but the whole human race, past, present, and future. (D2 246–47)

[GOD:] My only-begotten Son revealed to you through his pierced body the fire of my charity hidden under the ashes of your humanity. And would this not warm the frozen human heart? Yes, unless it is so obstinate and blinded by selfishness that it does not see how unspeakably much I love you. (D2 279)

[GOD:] In the blood I have made it clear that I do not want sinners to die, but rather to be converted and live. (D2 292)

[GOD:] Those who suffer themselves are far more compassionate to the suffering than are those who have not suffered. They grow to greater love and run to me all anointed with humility and ablaze in the furnace of my charity. (D2 305)

[GOD:] No pain will be so much rewarded, as mental pain and labour of the heart; for these are the greatest pains of all and therefore worthy of the greatest fruit. (C 48)

[GOD:] Out of his misery he gave you great wealth. From the narrow wood of the cross he extended his generosity to everyone. (D2 320)

[GOD:] The fiery chariot of my only-begotten Son came bringing the fire of my charity to your humanity with such overflowing mercy that the penalty for sins people commit was taken away. (D2 112)

[GOD:] The more the soul endures, the more she shows that she loves Me. (D1 38)

[C:] Let us endure, let us endure, . . . for the more pain we suffer down here with Christ crucified, the more glory shall we receive. (C 48)

[C:] Love held him fast. As the saints say, neither cross nor nails could have held him, were it not for the bond of divine charity. . . . Here you will discover and fall in love with true virtue. (L 15)

[C:] The Son runs to his death because of his longing to give us life; so great is his hunger and desire to obey his Father that he has set aside any selfish concern for himself and runs to the cross. (L 51)

[C:] He was like one in love on the cross, to show us that he loves us not for his own advantage but to make us holy. Truly he is there as our rule, as our way, as a book so written that any dull and blind person can read him. (L 93)

[C:] Mortify your body and don't pamper it with so much softness. Take yourself lightly; don't be concerned about nobility or wealth, because virtue is the only thing that makes one noble. (L 178)

[C:] Self-love . . . poisons the world! That is what has made you, who should be pillars, weaker than straw. (C 146)

[C:] Oh, what immeasurable grace you have received! For leaving behind the death of sin you have been given immortal life! (L 71)

THE
GLORIOUS
MYSTERIES

The First Glorious Mystery

The Resurrection of Jesus from the Dead

Faith

Blessed are those who have not seen and yet believe.
—John 20:29

[GOD:] I am the Infinite Good. (DI 59)

[GOD:] The precious Blood of My only-begotten Son
. . . destroyed death and darkness, and gave life and truth,
and confounded falsehood. (DI 66)

[GOD:] I will protect you, and My Providence shall never
fail you in the slightest need. (DI 73)

[GOD:] I also wish you to look at the Bridge of My
only-begotten Son, and see the greatness thereof. For
it reaches from Heaven to earth, that is, that the earth
of your humanity is joined to the greatness of the

Deity.... This Bridge reaches from Heaven to earth, and constitutes the union which I have made with man.

(D1 75)

[GOD:] How was Heaven opened? With the key of His Blood; so you see that the Bridge is walled and roofed with Mercy. (D1 81)

[GOD:] His doctrine is true, and has remained like a lifeboat to draw the soul out of the tempestuous sea and to conduct her to the port of salvation.... He is the Way, the Truth, and the Life; that is, the Bridge which leads you to the height of Heaven. (D1 87–88)

[GOD:] See then how He returns, not in actual flesh and blood, but ... building the road of His doctrine, with His power. [This] road cannot be destroyed or taken away from him who wishes to follow it, because it is firm and stable, and proceeds from Me, who am immovable. (D1 88)

[GOD:] I am the one who provides for everything whatever that may be needed for soul or body. In the measure that you put your trust in me, in that measure will my providence be meted out to you. (D2 226)

[GOD:] [The] light of faith enables the soul to discern, to know, and to follow the way and the doctrine of My Truth—the Word Incarnate; and without this pupil of faith she would not see. (D1 126)

[GOD:] Hold all things in reverence and at harvest time they [will] reap the fruit of their labors. (D2 286)

❦

[GOD:] If it is beauty you want, I am beauty. If you want goodness, I am goodness, for I am supremely good. I am wisdom. I am kind; I am compassionate; I am the just and merciful God. (D2 290)

[GOD:] The glorified humanity of My only-begotten Son ... gives you assurance of your resurrection. (D1 113)

[GOD:] His wounds ... have remained fresh, and the scars in His body are preserved, and continually cry for mercy for you, to Me, the Supreme and Eternal Father.
(D1 113–14)

[GOD:] The more they abandon themselves, the more they find me. (D2 304)

[GOD:] Men fall into false judgment. ... They are continually being scandalized by My works, which are all just and all performed in truth through love and mercy.
(D1 98–99)

[GOD:] You were all invited, generally and in particular, by My Truth when He cried in the Temple, saying: "Whosoever thirsts, let him come to Me and drink, for I am the Fountain of the Water of Life." (D1 134)

[G<small>OD</small>:] I loved you without being loved by you—before you existed. It was, indeed, love that moved Me to create you in My own image and [likeness]. (D1 194)

[G<small>OD</small>:] Rise above the feelings of your senses. (D1 206)

[G<small>OD</small>:] If the soul were … truly humble and not presumptuous, she would be illuminated to see that I, the Primary and Sweet Truth, grant condition, and time, and place, and consolations, and tribulations as they may be needed for your salvation, and to complete the perfection to which I have elected the soul. (D1 212)

[G<small>OD</small>:] He passed through like the true Captain and Knight that He was, whom I had placed on the battlefield to deliver you from the hands of the Devil, so that you might be free. (D1 214)

[G<small>OD</small>:] My will … wishes nothing else but your good; so that everything which I give or permit to happen to you I give so that you may arrive at the end for which I created you. (D1 220)

[G<small>OD</small>:] [Those] in a state of grace … see by faith and hold by love. (D1 264)

[G<small>OD</small>:] You know that every evil is grounded in selfish love of oneself. This love is a cloud that blots out the light of reason. It is in reason that the light of faith is held, and one cannot lose the one without losing the other. (D2 103)

[C:] Your Mercy caused your Son to do battle for us, hanging by His arms on the wood of the cross, life and death battling together; then life confounded the death of our sin, and the death of our sin destroyed the bodily life of the Immaculate Lamb. Which was finally conquered? Death! By what means? Mercy! Your Mercy gives light and life, by which Your clemency is known. (D1 90–91)

[C:] If God is with you, no one else shall be against you. It is God who moves you: therefore He is with you.
(C 110)

[C:] I confide in Our Lord Jesus Christ and not in men. . . . And if they give me infamy and persecution, I shall give tears and continual prayer, as God gives me grace. (C 125)

[C:] What you lack, God in His Goodness will supply.
(C 173)

[C:] If you had kept faith, you would not have wavered so much, nor fallen in doubt of God. (C 173)

[C:] God is happiness itself without a trace of sadness or bitterness, and God is wealth itself, never failing, safe from any thievery. (L 25)

[C:] O Gentle Jesus, it is really true that you are our peace, our tranquility, our serenity of conscience. No bitterness or sadness or poverty can touch the soul in whom you live by grace. (L 25)

[C:] Our heart can never find rest except in what is stable and secure. . . . So if we wish to have peace we must rest our heart and soul with faith and love in

Christ crucified. Only then will our soul find complete happiness. (L 27)

[C:] God cannot will anything but our good. (L 27)

[C:] Truly nothing happens to us except God's will and permission—death or life, sickness or health, riches or poverty, even the wrongs done us by friends or relatives or anyone else. Not a leaf falls from a tree without his consent. (L 28)

[C:] I long to see in you the same power of holy faith and perseverance as the Canaanite woman had. She had such a strong faith that she won her daughter's deliverance from the devil. Even more, God wanted to show how pleased he was with her faith. (L 65)

[C:] Only Christ crucified was the Lamb who with unspeakable love opened up his slain body, giving himself to us as bath and as medicine, as food and as garment and as a bed where we can rest. (L 177)

[C:] I want your security to be in Christ gentle Jesus. He has clothed us in the sturdiest garment there is, a garment of love. . . . The very first garment we ever had was love, for it was only by love that we were created in God's image and likeness. (L 185–86)

[C:] God gives us what we can bear, and no more. . . . If you believe that God wants only our good, you will stay perfectly happy. Be comforted in Christ crucified, and don't be afraid. (L 28)

[C:] Oh sweet life-giving faith! If you persevere in that faith, sadness will never overtake your heart. For sadness comes only from putting our trust in creatures. . . . So if we wish to have peace we must rest our heart and soul with faith and love in Christ. (L 27)

[C:] Oh gentlest eternal Truth, give us huge mouthfuls to eat! I can do no more than invite you, in the name of Christ crucified, to provision the ship of your soul with hunger and faith. (L 195)

[C:] Christ is as powerful now as then, for he never changes. (L 229)

[C:] The love of God and of holy virtue is a light that frees us from all the darkness of ignorance. It gives us life and frees us from death. It gives us strength, security, and stability. (L 240)

[C:] If a father has many children and only one remains faithful to him, the father will give that child the inheritance. I tell you, even if you should be all alone, stand firm on this battlefield and don't turn back. (L 243)

[C:] A person who walks with a lamp at night doesn't stumble. Souls who have God as their lamp cannot stumble either. . . . Because of their will and desire to follow their Master, they run on attentively and eagerly. (L 258)

The Second Glorious Mystery

The Ascension of Jesus into Heaven

Hope

Ask, and it will be given you; seek, and you will find; knock, and it will be opened to you.—Luke 11:9

[GOD:] The eye cannot see, nor the tongue relate, nor the heart think, how many are the roads and ways which I use, through love alone, to lead them back to grace, so that My truth may be fulfilled in them. (D1 35)

[GOD:] I say to you all, that you should ask, and it will be given you. For I deny nothing to him who asks of Me in truth. (D1 38–39)

[GOD:] I have everlasting life to reward you in myself. (D2 95)

[GOD:] I have made a Bridge of My Word, of My only-begotten Son, and this is the truth. (D1 73)

[GOD:] If they are prudent, constant, and persevering, they will succeed. (D2 113)

[GOD:] The way of the Truth . . . leads to life with a perfect light. (D1 87)

[GOD:] The soul's being and capacity to love are infinite. . . . If you end in love of virtue you will receive an infinite reward. (D2 176)

[GOD:] In His bodily presence He will not return until the last Day of Judgment, when He will come again with My Majesty and Divine Power to judge the world, to render good to the virtuous and reward them for their labors, both in body and soul. (D1 89)

[GOD:] I for my part will fulfill your desires. But never fail—neither you nor they—to trust me, for my providence will not fail you. (D2 204)

[GOD:] Either [the soul] must serve and hope in me, or she will serve and hope in the world and herself. (D2 280)

[GOD:] It is not the body that gives bliss to the soul, but the soul will give bliss to the body, because the soul will give of her abundance, and will re-clothe herself on the Last Day of Judgment, in the garments of her own flesh.
(D1 112–13)

[GOD:] They that love Me . . . understand by the light of faith that good must be rewarded. (D1 127–28)

[GOD:] I never fail those who never fail in their hope. I provide for them as a kind compassionate father. (D2 322)

[GOD:] You are invited to the Fountain of the Living Water of Grace. (D1 134–35)

[GOD:] My goodness ... is never withheld from him who will receive it. (D1 163)

[GOD:] The Devil [is not] able to resist your humble hope in My goodness. (D1 163)

[GOD:] The Eternal Deity drew to Himself the pain, which I suffered with so much fire and love.... The fruit, which came out of the pain and desire for your salvation, is infinite, and therefore you receive it infinitely. Had it not been infinite, the whole human generation could not have been restored to grace. (D1 174)

[GOD:] In the opening of My Side ... is found the secret of the Heart, showing that I loved more than I could show with finite pain. (D1 174)

[GOD:] I showed to you that My love was infinite. How? By the Baptism of Blood united with the fire of My charity.... And in order to show this, it was necessary for the Blood to come out of My Side. (D1 174)

[GOD:] Rise out of yourself, and open the eye of your intellect to see Me, the Infinite Goodness, and the ineffable love which I have towards you and My other servants. (D1 206)

[GOD:] My Providence will never fail you, and every man, if he be humble, shall receive that which he is fit to receive. (D1 227)

[GOD:] I will fulfill your desires, but do not fail . . . in your hope in me. My Providence will never fail you, and every man, if he be humble shall receive that which he is fit to . . . receive from My goodness. (D1 227)

[GOD:] I, God, have become man. And man has become God by the union of My Divine Nature with your human nature. This greatness is given in general to all. (D1 228)

[GOD:] The hope with which they have lived, confiding in My providence and losing all trust in themselves . . . causes them now with delight to lift their confidence towards Me. (D1 262–63)

[GOD:] I wish [souls] to hope in My mercy at the point of death. . . . During their life I use this sweet trick with them, making them hope greatly in My mercy. (D1 268)

[GOD:] Inasmuch as I am the Supreme Truth, I will keep My word, fulfilling the promise which I made to you, and satisfying your [holy] desire. (D1 281)

[GOD:] I, in this life, will give you a hundredfold for one.   (D1 312)

[GOD:] I wish to do mercy to the world, proving to you that mercy is My special attribute, for through the mercy and the inestimable love which I had for man, I sent to the earth the Word, My only-begotten Son.   (D1 326)

[C:] You, Eternal Trinity, are my Creator, and I am the work of Your hands, and I know through the new creation which You have given me in the blood of Your Son, that You are enamored of the beauty of Your workmanship. Oh! Abyss, oh! Eternal Godhead! oh! Sea Profound! what more could You give me than Yourself?
(D1 332)

[C:] The heart of man knows not how to ask or desire as much as You can give, and thus I see that You are He who is the Supreme and Eternal Good.   (D1 276)

[C:] To You, Eternal Father, everything is possible.
(D1 280)

[C:] God will refresh you. Great consolation follows a great trial.   (C 183)

[C:] Clothe, clothe yourself with Christ crucified. He is the wedding garment that will give you grace here, and afterward will afford you a place with the true feasters at the table of everlasting life.   (L 16)

[C:] You will show that you are indeed alive when you harmonize and unite your will with God's. This sweet will of his will give you living faith and hope set entirely on God. (L 27)

[C:] Put your hope decisively in God and not in this mortal life. I beg you, as ransomed servants, to set your desire and your soul's affection intently on your Savior who has ransomed you. (L 30)

[C:] Of ourselves we are all so weak and frail that we fall at the slightest obstacle. But divine providence is at work within our soul, strengthening us and relieving us of all weakness. So be trustful, firmly believing that God always provides for souls who trust in him. (L 76)

[C:] It was for love only, and not because he had to, that he drew us out of himself. We never asked him to create us but moved by the fire of his charity he did, so that we might experience and enjoy his supreme eternal beauty. (L 99)

[C:] He is the peaceful sea that provides drink for all who thirst, for all who hunger and long for God. He gives peace to all who have been at war, yet want to be reconciled with him. This sea pours out a fire that warms every cold heart. (L 106)

[C:] See how God loves you! Words could not describe, nor your heart imagine, nor your eyes see how great are the graces he wants to pour out on you. . . . Be grateful and appreciative, so that the fountain of piety may not dry up within you. (L 138)

[C:] [He] pours the gift of his blazing charity into your souls. This is the sweet hundredfold; without it we could not have eternal life, and with it everlasting life cannot be taken away from us. (L 222)

[C:] He is such a loving companion to souls who follow him that when we reach the end in death he puts us to rest in that bed, that peaceful sea of divine Being, where we receive the eternal vision of God. (L 235)

[C:] May we always see ourselves in the incarnate Word, God's only-begotten Son, as in a mirror, for he was way and rule for us, and if we keep this way and rule it will always give us life. (L 259)

THE THIRD GLORIOUS MYSTERY

THE DESCENT OF THE HOLY SPIRIT

Love of God

(Y)ou shall love the Lord your God with all your heart, and with all your soul, and with all your mind, and with all your strength.— Mark 12:30

[GOD:] Charity gives life to all the virtues, because no virtue can be obtained without charity, which is the pure love of Me. (D1 44)

[GOD:] I wish for no other thing than love, for in the love of Me is fulfilled and completed the love of the neighbor, and the law observed. For he, only, can be of use in his state of life, who is bound to Me with this love. (D1 47)

[GOD:] Love should be directed to Me endlessly, bound-lessly, since I am the Supreme and Eternal Truth. (D1 58)

[GOD:] He drew everything to Himself . . . by showing the ineffable love with which I love you, the heart of man being always attracted by love. Greater love, then, I could not show you, than to lay down My life for you. (D1 79)

[GOD:] I will dwell in your souls by grace and be with you on your journey. (D2 107)

[GOD:] When He ... had thus ascended on high, and returned to Me the Father, I sent the Master, that is the Holy Spirit, who came to you with My power and the wisdom of My Son, and with His own clemency, which is the essence of the Holy Spirit. (D1 85)

[GOD:] The Holy Spirit gives [Jesus' follower] love which consumes and takes away all [sensual] love out of the soul, leaving there only the love of virtue. (D1 87–88)

[GOD:] The soul cannot live without love, but always wants to love something, because she is made of love, and, by love, I created her. (D1 130)

[GOD:] Love transforms the lover into the object loved, and where two friends have one soul there can be no secret between them, wherefore My Truth said: "I will come and we will dwell together," and this is the truth. (D1 146)

[GOD:] Do you know how I manifest Myself to the soul who loves Me in truth, and follows the doctrine of My sweet and amorous Word? (D1 146)

❧

[GOD:] By love you are made, and had My love been drawn back, that is, had I not loved your being, you could not be. But My love created you, and My love possesses you. (D1 178)

[G<small>OD</small>:] The soul that desires Me possesses Me in very truth. (D1 198)

[G<small>OD</small>:] The soul touches Me with the hand of love. (D1 237)

[G<small>OD</small>:] He who knows more loves Me more, and he who loves Me more receives more. Your reward is measured according to the measure of your love. (D1 262)

[G<small>OD</small>:] Love cannot be alone, but is accompanied by all the true and royal virtues, because all the virtues draw their life from love. (D1 283)

[G<small>OD</small>:] Charity alone enters into eternal life, like a mistress bringing with her the fruit of all the other virtues, while they remain outside, bringing their fruit into Me, the eternal life, in whom the obedient taste eternal life. (D1 313)

[G<small>OD</small>:] Charity is an open book to be read by all. (D1 313)

[G<small>OD</small>:] The Holy Spirit, my loving charity, is the waiter who serves them my gifts and graces. This gentle waiter carries to me their tender loving desires, and carries back to them the reward for their labors, the sweetness of my charity for their enjoyment and nourishment. (D2 146)

[God:] Every man will receive a price, according to the measure of his love, and not according to the work he does, or the length of time for which he works. . . . He who comes early will not have more than he who comes late, as My Truth told you in the holy gospel. (Dᵢ 320)

[C:] You, oh eternal Trinity, are a deep Sea, into which the deeper I enter the more I find, and the more I find the more I seek; the soul cannot be satiated in Your abyss, for she continually hungers after You, the eternal Trinity. (Dᵢ 331)

[C:] No soul could look at God becoming a man, running to the shame of the holy cross, and shedding his blood so profusely, and not draw near, enter in, and be filled with true love. (L 21)

[C:] The soul unites herself with God by the affection of love. (Dᵢ 27)

[C:] Oh fire, oh abyss of charity! You are a fire ever burning but not consuming. You are filled with gladness, with rejoicing, with gentleness. To the heart pierced by this arrow, all bitterness seems sweet, every heavy burden becomes light. (L 38)

[C:] [The abyss of charity] burns and consumes. It dissolves and destroys all sin, all ignorance, all indifference in the soul, for charity is not lazy. No, it does great things! (L 39)

[C:] Oh splendid glorious virtue! It is you that reveal the presence of the fire of divine charity within the soul, for people have faith and hope only in what they love. These three virtues flow from one another. (L 65)

[C:] There is no love without faith, nor faith without hope. They are the three pillars that uphold the fortress of our soul so firmly. . . . It will be supported by these three dependable pillars. (L 65)

[C:] Let our hearts and souls burst with love! Let them be quick to serve and stand in awe of the good gentle Jesus! . . . Jesus rescued us. He assumed responsibility for us, paid our debt, and then tore up the bond. (L 66)

[C:] I think of that Spirit as the love that dissipates all darkness and gives perfect light, that supplants all ignorance with perfect knowledge. (L 166)

[C:] We should do as a loving person does when a friend comes with a gift, not looking at the friend's hands to see what the gift is, but looking with the eyes of love at the friend's loving heart. And this is what God's supreme, eternal, more tender than tender goodness wants us to do when he visits our soul. (L 96)

[C:] We are like a field where God in his mercy has sown his seed, the love and affection with which he created us. . . . And to nourish the plants and make this seed bear fruit, he gave us the water of holy baptism. (L 99)

[C:] It is nature and the power of love that compel a true child to love and serve a father. Such, I tell you, should be our love for our heavenly Father. . . . He is supreme and just and eternally good, and for his infinite goodness he deserves to be loved. (L 123)

[C:] Those who see how boundlessly God loves them cannot refrain from loving, because it is the nature of love to love what the beloved loves. (L 167)

[C:] We cannot exist without love since we are made of nothing less than love. Whatever we have, physically or spiritually, we have because of love—for it is by love alone, with the help of God's grace, that a mother and a father give their child existence. (L 186)

[C:] They can have as much grace as they want whenever they want it—not by their own power, though, but by grace itself, the gift of the Holy Spirit. (L 187)

[C:] It seems to me every one of us should go—even on all fours if we can't walk upright—to demonstrate our love for him by giving him our lives for love of Life, to use our bodies to expiate our sins and failings just as we have used our bodies to offend. (L 189)

[C:] Love is had only by loving. If you want love, you must begin by loving—I mean you must want to love. Once you want it, you must open the eye of your understanding to see where and how love is to be found. (L 204)

[C:] Everything we have, everything we discover within ourselves, is indeed the gift of God's boundless goodness and charity. . . . This is love's way, that when we see ourselves loved we love in return. (L 205)

[C:] God's love for our souls was the rock and the nails that held him fast. This then is how we find love should be: And how are we to love once we have discovered where love is? . . . He himself is the rule and the way. There is no other. (L 205)

[C:] When . . . our affection and love are turned away from ourselves and centered entirely in Christ crucified, we achieve the greatest dignity possible to us, because we become one with our Creator. (L 207)

[C:] The soul who has fallen in love with God, she who is a servant and slave ransomed by the blood of God's Son, attains such great dignity that she cannot be called a servant now, but an empress, spouse of the eternal emperor! (L 208)

[C:] Love God not for your own sake, for your own profit, but love him for his sake, because he is the highest Good and is worthy of being loved. Then your love will be perfect and not mercenary. (L 209)

[C:] If he had not so fallen in love with you he would never have created you. But because of the love he had for you as he saw you within himself, he was moved to grant you being. How your thoughts will be stretched when you drink this charity! (L 209)

[C:] Love, that is, the Holy Spirit, sustains everything. The Holy Spirit is the light that banishes all darkness, the hand that upholds the whole world. (L 234)

[C:] The fire of divine charity does to our soul what physical fire does: it warms us, enlightens us, changes us into itself. Oh gentle and fascinating fire! You warm and you drive out the cold of vice and sin and self-centeredness! (L 266)

The Fourth Glorious Mystery

The Assumption of Mary into Heaven

Desire for Heaven

*Come, O blessed of my Father, inherit the kingdom prepared
for you from the foundation of the world.* — Matthew 25:34

[God:] Eternal life, the vision of peace and supreme
eternal tranquility and rest—[is] an immeasurable reward.
No one can imagine how great it is, because it is infinite.

(D2 359–60)

[God:] I had created them in my image and likeness so
that they might have eternal life, sharing in my being and
enjoying my supreme eternal tenderness and goodness.

(D2 58)

[God:] The height of the Divinity, humbled to the earth
and joined with your humanity, made the Bridge and
reformed the road. Why was this done? In order that
man might come to his true happiness with the angels.

(D1 76)

[God:] The saints exult in the sight of Me, refreshing
themselves with joyousness in the fruit of their toils borne
for Me with such abundance of love. (D1 105)

[GOD:] The just soul, for whom life finishes in the affection of charity and the bonds of love, cannot increase in virtue, time having come to nought, but she can always love with that affection with which she comes to Me, and that measure that is measured to her. (D1 110)

[GOD:] [The just souls will] rejoice and exult with the angels, and they find their places among the saints according to the different virtues in which they excelled in the world.... For when a soul reaches eternal life, all share in her good and she in theirs. (D2 83)

[GOD:] I call the soul "heaven" because I make heaven wherever I dwell by grace. I made the soul my hiding place and by my love turned her into a mansion. (D2 75)

[GOD:] In those bonds of love in which [the blessed] finished their life, they go on and remain eternally. They are conformed so entirely to my will, that they cannot desire except what I desire.... Their desires are all satisfied. (D1 112)

[GOD:] The eye of your intellect is not sufficient to see, nor your ear to hear, nor your tongue to tell of the good of the Blessed. Oh, how much delight they have in seeing Me, who am every good! (D1 113)

[GOD:] I send people troubles in this world so that they may know that their goal is not this life, and that these things are imperfect and passing. I am their goal, and I want them to want me, and in this spirit they should accept such things. (D2 100)

❦

[GOD:] You will all be conformed with Him, eye with eye, and hand with hand, and with the whole Body of the sweet Word My Son, and, dwelling in Me, you will dwell in Him, because He is one thing with Me. (D1 114)

[GOD:] Every work, good or bad, is done by means of the body. And, therefore, justly, My daughter, glory and infinite good are rendered to My elect ones with their glorified body, rewarding them for the toils they bore for Me, together with the soul. (D1 116)

[GOD:] Do you know what is the special good of the blessed ones? It is having their desire filled with what they desire; wherefore desiring Me, they have Me. (D1 125)

[GOD:] Filial love, I tell you, is perfect. For with filial love one receives the inheritance from me, the eternal Father. But no one attains filial love without the love of friendship, and this is why I told you that one progresses from being my friend to becoming my child. (D2 118)

[GOD:] After the soul has left the weight of the body, her desire is full, for, desiring to see Me, she sees Me, in which vision is her bliss; and seeing she knows, and knowing she loves, and loving she tastes Me, Supreme and Eternal Good. (D1 125)

[GOD:] I told you that the tasting of eternal life consisted especially in having that which the will desires. (D1 126)

[GOD:] You have nothing infinite except your soul's love and desire. (D2 170)

[GOD:] Seeing Me, the Eternal Father, [the soul] loves. And loving, she is satisfied. Satisfied, she knows the Truth, and her will is stayed in My Will, bound and made stable, so that in nothing can it suffer pain, because it has that which it desired to have. (D1 177)

[GOD:] [Blessed souls] desire to come and be with Me. (D1 180)

[GOD:] The souls in the unitive state love Me, because love follows the intellect, and the more it knows the more can it love. Thus the one feeds the other, and, with this light, they both arrive at the Eternal Vision of Me, where they see and taste Me in Truth. (D1 185)

[GOD:] Suffering has ended for the blessed, but not love. (D2 151)

[GOD:] [The enamored soul] expects perfection in immortal life. (D1 222)

[GOD:] They taste peace without any disturbance; they receive and clothe themselves in the most perfect peace, for there they possess every good without any evil, safety

without any fear, riches without any poverty ... one supreme infinite good, shared by all those who taste it.
(D1 291)

[GOD:] Being the infinite good, [eternal life] cannot be understood by anything smaller than itself, like a vessel, which dipped into the sea, does not comprehend the whole sea, but only that quantity which it contains. (D1 325)

[GOD:] The sea alone contains itself. So I, the Sea Pacific, am He who alone can comprehend and value Myself truly. . . . This joy, the good which I have in Myself, I share with you and with all, according to the measure of each. (D1 325)

[GOD:] I do not leave you empty, but fill you, giving you perfect beatitude; each man comprehends and knows My goodness in the measure in which it is given to him.
(D1 325)

[GOD:] [Those who remove spiritual selfishness] see that everything comes from me, that not a leaf falls from the tree apart from my providence, and that I give and permit what I do for their sanctification, so that they may have the final good for which I created all of you. (D2 114)

[GOD:] The truth is that I created you in order to possess eternal life, and manifested this with the blood of My only-begotten Son, the Word. (D1 328–29)

[God:] The tongue would not be sufficient to relate the delight felt by him who goes on this road, for even in this life, he tastes and participates in that good which has been prepared for him in eternal life. (D1 84)

[C:] God is the placid sea in which His creatures may lose themselves; He is the boundless sea; the sea of light; the fathomless sea. (C 81)

[C:] Realize that in this life we, like the Canaanite woman, can have only the crumbs that fall from the table—I mean the graces we receive, that fall from the Lord's table. But when we reach everlasting life, where we will see God face to face and will taste him, the food on the table will be ours. So never evade hard work. (L 67)

[C:] What peace, what calm, what sweetness our soul receives and enjoys once we have come home to port and have found the slain Lamb whom we had sought on the cross and who is now our table, our food, and our servant! (L 77)

[C:] Courage, my dear brother, for soon we shall reach the wedding feast. (L 87)

[C:] I beg you, for the love of Christ crucified, let your soul's eye be directed toward God in all that you do. Oh what great joy and happiness you will feel when the time comes for you to be called by First Truth, knowing that you are in the company of the virtues. (L 116)

[C:] Ablaze with the fire of love may you go forward from ... this poor fleeting life to that eternal city of Jerusalem, the vision of peace, where divine mercy will make us all kings and queens, lords and ladies. (L 149)

[C:] The soul who has discovered love in the love of Christ ... will prefer to be like a pilgrim or traveler in this life, with her attention focused wholly on reaching her journey's goal. And if she is a good pilgrim, neither any prosperity she may encounter along the way nor any difficulty will slow her down. (L 206)

[C:] The reason we cannot have this sort of peace in this life is that our desire is not completely satisfied until we reach this union with the divine Being. As long as we are pilgrim travelers in this life we have only desire and hunger: desire to follow the right path, and hunger to reach our final destination. (L 208)

[C:] Oh how lovely and happy our souls will be when our time comes to be called by gentle First Truth at the sweet moment of death, when we shall be exultantly happy to see ourselves dressed in the garment of divine grace! (L 218)

[C:] Where Christ is, life eternal should be. (C 148)

The Fifth Glorious Mystery

The Crowning of Mary Queen of Heaven and Earth

Devotion to Mary

Behold, your mother!
—John 19:27

[God:] I had not forgotten the reverence and love he had for Mary, my only-begotten Son's most gentle mother. (D2 286)

[God:] My goodness, in deference to the Word, has decreed that anyone at all, just or sinner, who holds her in due reverence will never be snatched or devoured by the infernal demon. (D2 286)

[God:] She is like a bait set out by my goodness to catch [souls]. (D2 286)

[God:] He [St. Dominic] was a light that I offered the world through Mary and sent into the mystic body of holy Church as an uprooter of heresies. . . . Mary gave him the habit—a task my goodness entrusted to her. (D2 337)

[GOD:] You see this gentle loving Word born in a stable while Mary was on a journey, to show you pilgrims how you should be constantly born anew in the stable of self-knowledge, where by grace you will find me born within your soul. (D2 320)

[C:] All of you pray to God and Our Lady to send us good results. (C 123)

[C:] Be a man; make haste; respond to Mary who is calling you with such great love. (C 171)

[C:] Offer yourselves first thing morning and night to that sweet mother Mary, praying her to be your advocate and protectress. (C 180)

[C:] In that sweet and blessed field of Mary, the Word made flesh was like the grain which is ripened by the warm rays of the sun, and puts forth its flowers and fruit, letting its husk fall to the earth. (A 1)

[C:] Warmed by the fire of Divine Charity, He cast the seed of the Word into the field of Mary. (A 1)

❦

[C:] O Blessed Mary! It was you who gave us the flower of our sweetest Jesus. That flower yielded its fruit on the Holy Cross, because there it was that we received the gift of perfect life. (A 1)

[C:] O sweetest love, this was the sword that struck your mother's heart and soul. The Son was physically pierced, and so was his mother, since his flesh was hers. This was only right, since that flesh was her own: he had taken his flesh from her. (L 50)

[C:] O fire of charity!—I see another union here. He now has the form of flesh, and she like warm wax has received from the seal of the Holy Spirit the imprint of loving desire for our salvation. By that seal and engrafting the eternal divine Word became incarnate. (L 50)

[C:] Willingly she gives up her [natural] love for her Son. Not only does she not, as a mother would, deter him from death, but she would [even be willing to] make herself the ladder; she *wants* him to die. This is no surprise, though, for she has been wounded by the arrow of love for our salvation. (L 51)

[C:] Oh blessed gentle Mary! She gave us the gentle Jesus as a blossom. And when did that blessed blossom produce fruit? When he was engrafted onto the wood of the most holy cross—then we received perfect life. (L 104)

[C:] She could desire nothing but God's honor and the salvation of his creatures. . . . She would have made a ladder of her very self to put her Son on the cross if there had been no other way. All this was because her Son's will remained within her. (L 105)

[C:] Never let it leave your heart and soul and memory that you were offered and presented to Mary. Ask her then to offer and present you to Jesus, her gentle Son, and she, kind and gentle mother of mercy that she is, will do it. (L 105)

[C:] Run on courageously, gently driven as Mary was—I mean seeking always God's honor and the salvation of souls. (L 105)

[C:] Put up no more resistance to the Holy Spirit who is calling you, and do not spurn Mary's love for you or the prayers and tears that are being poured out for you. (L 282)

[C:] Have recourse to that dear Mary, mother of mercy and compassion. She will lead you into her Son's presence ... and so persuade him to be merciful to you. (L 292)

[C:] Look! Look at the ineffable love God is offering you! Look at the sweetness of the tender fruit, the spotless Lamb, the seed sown in Mary as in a lovely field! (L 101)

[C:] Human pride must really blush to see God so humbled in gentle Mary's womb. She was the field in which the seed of the incarnate Word, God's Son, was sown. (L 104)

[C:] The Son runs to his death because of his longing to give us life; so great is his hunger and desire to obey his Father that he has set aside any selfish concern for himself and runs to the cross. And his dearest gentlest mother does the same. (L 51)

[C:] I am confident that, through the overflowing blood of Jesus Christ and by the merits of these saints and of that most gentle mother, we too will enter into the vision and very being of God, where we will see and enjoy Christ face to face. (L 54)

[C:] O Mary! Mary! Temple of the Trinity! O Mary, bearer of the fire! Mary, minister of mercy! Mary, seed bed of the fruit! . . . The world was redeemed when in the Word your own flesh suffered: Christ by his passion redeemed us; you, by your grief of body and spirit. (P 185–86)

[C:] O Mary, peaceful sea! Mary, giver of peace! Mary, fertile soil! You, Mary, are the new-sprung plant from whom we have the fragrant blossom, the Word, God's only-begotten Son, for in you, fertile soil, was this Word sown. (P 186)

[C:] O Mary, vessel of humility! In you the light of true knowledge thrives and burns. By this light you rose above yourself, and so you were pleasing to the eternal Father, and he seized you and drew you to himself, loving you with a special love. (P 186)

[C:] I say that our human dignity is revealed because if I look at you, Mary, I see that the Holy Spirit's hand has written the Trinity in you by forming within you the incarnate Word, God's only-begotten Son. (P 188)

[C:] O Mary, I see this Word given to you, living in you yet not separated from the Father—just as the word one has in one's mind does not leave one's heart or become separated from it even though that word is externalized and communicated to others. In these things our human dignity is revealed. (P 191)

[C:] The eternal Godhead, O Mary, was knocking at your door, but unless you had opened that door of your will God would not have taken flesh in you. Blush, my soul, when you see today God has become your relative in Mary. (P 193)

[C:] O Mary, my tenderest love! In you is written the Word from whom we have the teaching of life. You are the tablet that sets this teaching before us. (P 193)

[C:] O Mary, may you be proclaimed blessed among all women for endless ages, . . . you have shared with us your flour. . . . The Godhead is joined and kneaded into one dough with our humanity—so securely that this union could never be broken, either by death or by our thanklessness. (P 195)

[C:] The bridegroom was joined with his bride—the divinity in the Word with our humanity—and the medium of this union was Mary, who clothed you, the eternal bridegroom, in her humanity. (P 205–6)

[C:] The eternal Word is given to us through Mary's hands. From Mary's substance he clothed himself in our nature without the stain of original sin—for that conception was not a man's doing, but the Holy Spirit's. (P 242)

[C:] The law of love arrived because God's Son came in the Virgin Mary and shed his blood so lavishly in the wood of the most holy cross, we are able to receive the lavish flow of divine mercy. (L 282)

OTHER
TOPICS

Prayer

Watch and pray that you may not enter into temptation.
—Mark 14:38

[GOD:] [The soul] awaits, with lively faith, the coming of the Holy Spirit, that is of Me, who am the fire of charity. How does she await me? Not in idleness, but in watching and continued prayer. (D1 153)

[GOD:] I accept from you your restless desires, your tears and sighs, your constant humble prayers. (D2 46)

[GOD:] They seek me in prayer, wanting to know my power, and I satisfy them by letting them taste and feel my strength. (D2 116)

[GOD:] [The soul] continues to pray with the prayer of holy desire, which is a continued prayer. (D1 154)

[GOD:] Prayer is a weapon with which you can defend yourself against every enemy. If you hold it with love's hand and the arm of free choice, this weapon, with the light of most holy faith, will be your defense. (D2 122)

[GOD:] During the time ordained for prayer the Devil is wont to arrive in the soul, causing much more conflict and trouble than when the soul is not occupied in prayer. This he does in order that holy prayer may become tedious to the soul. (D1 158–59)

[GOD:] Know, dearest daughter, how by humble, continual and faithful prayer the soul acquires with time and perseverance, every virtue. Wherefore should she persevere and never abandon prayer. (D1 159)

[GOD:] Oh, how sweet and pleasant to that soul and to Me is holy prayer, made in the house of knowledge of self and of Me, opening the eye of the intellect to the light of faith, and the affections to the abundance of My charity. (D1 160)

[GOD:] [The soul] should not say her vocal prayers without joining them to mental prayer, that is to say, that while she is reciting, she should endeavor to elevate her mind in My love. (D1 161–62)

[GOD:] A person has to walk step by step. . . . She should certainly, while she is still imperfect, stay with vocal prayer so as not to fall into laziness, but she should not omit mental prayer. In other words, while she says the words she should make an effort to concentrate on my love, pondering at the same time her own sins and the blood of my only-begotten Son. (D2 124)

[GOD:] Vocal prayer will profit the soul who practices it and it will please me. And if she perseveres in its practice, she will advance from imperfect vocal prayer to perfect mental prayer. (D2 125)

[GOD:] Charity is itself continual prayer. (D1 167)

[GOD:] As soon as she senses her spirit ready for my visitation, she ought to abandon vocal prayer. Then, after the mental prayer, if she has time, she can resume what she had set herself to say.... The Divine Office is an exception to this. (D2 126)

[GOD:] Vocal prayer, made in the way I have told you, will enable the soul to arrive at perfection, and therefore she should not abandon it, but use it in the way I have told you. (D1 165)

[GOD:] Perfect prayer is not attained to through many words but through affection of desire, the soul raising herself to Me, with knowledge of herself and of My mercy, seasoned the one with the other. (D1 166)

[GOD:] As far as concerns any other prayer the soul might begin, she ought to begin vocally as a way to reach mental prayer. When she senses that her spirit is ready she should abandon vocal prayer with this intent. Such prayer, made in the way I have told you, will bring her to perfection. (D2 126)

[GOD:] [A person should] exercise together mental and vocal prayer, for, even as the active and contemplative life is one, so are they. (D1 166)

[GOD:] Holy desire, that is, having a good and holy will, is continual prayer. (D2 126)

[GOD:] Each one, according to his condition, ought to exert himself for the salvation of souls, for this exercise lies at the root of a holy will, and whatever he may contribute, by words or deeds, towards the salvation of his neighbor, is virtually a prayer. (D1 166)

[GOD:] Everything you do can be a prayer, whether in itself or in the form of charity to your neighbors. (D2 127)

[GOD:] Every time and place is for [perfect ones] a time and place of prayer. (D2 145)

[GOD:] Offer prayers for all people and for the mystic body of holy Church and for those I have given you to love with a special love. Do not be guilty of indifference about offering prayers and the example of your living. (D2 204)

[GOD:] My glorious apostle Paul . . . abandoned his infidelity, and the persecutions he directed against the Christians, at the prayer of St. Stephen. (D1 200)

[GOD:] Oh, how lovely, how lovely beyond all loveliness, is the dwelling place of the soul's perfect union with me! . . . She gives forth a fragrance to the whole wide world, the fruit of constant humble prayers. (D2 181)

[God:] I beg you to pray to me for them. I ask for your tears and sweat on their behalf so that they may receive mercy from me. (D2 71)

[God:] [The obedient] avoid idleness by constant humble prayer. (D2 344)

[God:] The glorious Thomas Aquinas ... gained his knowledge more from the study of prayer and the lifting up of his mind and the light of understanding than from human study. (D2 181)

[C:] The medicine by which he willed to heal the whole world and to soothe his wrath and divine justice was humble, constant, holy prayer. (D2 57)

[C:] You cause them to cry in order to hear their voices! Your Truth told us to cry out, and we should be answered; to knock, and it would be opened to us; to beg, and it would be given to us. (D1 278)

[C:] Pray the prayer of action, which is the fragrant flowering of the soul. A good man *is* a prayer. (C 48)

[C:] Prayer ... unites with God the soul that follows the footprints of Christ Crucified. (D1 26)

[C:] I beg of you not to cease praying; indeed, redouble it. (C 132)

[C:] I am sure that God's goodness will not make light of your prayers. (L 161)

[C:] Take courage, because God will not scorn the tears and sweat and sighs poured out in his presence. . . . Among the thorns I smell the fragrance of the rose about to open.
(L 182–83)

[C:] There is no way [a soul] can so savor and be enlightened by this truth as in continual humble prayer, grounded in the knowledge of herself and of God. For by such prayer the soul is united with God, following in the footsteps of Christ crucified. (D2 25)

The Eucharist

*He who eats my flesh and drinks my blood has eternal life,
and I will raise him up at the last day.*—John 6:54

[GOD:] In communion the souls seems more sweetly bound to God and better knows his truth. For then the soul is in God and God in the soul, just as the fish is in the sea and the sea in the fish. (D2 27)

[GOD:] I give this Blood and use It for salvation and perfection in the case of that man who disposes himself properly to receive it, for It gives life and adorns the soul with every grace, in proportion to the disposition and affection of him who receives It. (D1 66)

[GOD:] He says he is Truth, and so he is, and whoever follows him goes the way of truth. And he is Life. If you follow this truth you will have the life of grace and never die of hunger, for the Word has himself become your food. (D2 67)

[GOD:] [His] Blood inebriates the soul and clothes her with the fire of charity, giving her the food of the Sacrament which is placed in the tavern of the mystical body of the Holy Church. That is to say, the food of the Body & Blood of My Son, wholly God and wholly man. (D1 160)

[G<small>OD</small>:] This is the hostel [Holy Church] I had mentioned to you that stands on the bridge to dispense the food to strengthen the pilgrim travelers who go the way of my Truth's teaching, so that weakness will not cause them to fall. (D2 123)

[G<small>OD</small>:] I am the flawless Food of Life. (D1 221)

[G<small>OD</small>:] Go into battle filled and inebriated with the blood of Christ crucified. My charity sets this blood before you in the hostel of the mystic body of holy Church to give courage to those who would be true knights and fight against their selfish sensuality and weak flesh. (D2 143)

[G<small>OD</small>:] It is the whole divine being that you receive in that most gracious sacrament under that whiteness of bread. And just as the sun cannot be divided, so neither can my wholeness as God and as human in this white host. (D2 207)

[G<small>OD</small>:] This Body is, as it were, a Sun. Wherefore, you cannot receive the Body without the Blood, or the Blood or the Body without the Soul of the Incarnate Word; nor the Soul, nor the Body, without the Divinity of Me, the Eternal God. (D1 230)

[G<small>OD</small>:] The Divine Nature never left the human nature, either by death or from any other cause. So that you receive the whole Divine Essence in that most Sweet Sacrament concealed under the whiteness of the bread.
(D1 230)

[GOD:] Contemplate the marvelous state of the soul who receives this bread of life, this food of angels, as she ought. When she receives this sacrament she lives in me and I in her. Just as the fish is in the sea and the sea in the fish, so am I in the soul and the soul in me, the sea of peace.
(D2 211)

[GOD:] As the sun cannot be divided into light, heat, and color, the whole of God and the whole of man cannot be separated under the white mantle of the host. Even if the host should be divided into a million particles (if it were possible) in each particle should I be present, whole God and whole Man. (D1 230)

[GOD:] You could receive no greater gift than that I should give you myself, wholly God and wholly human, as your food. (D2 216)

[GOD:] You should reflect that, were it possible for the angels to be purified, they would have to be purified for this mystery. . . . I am telling you this to make you see what great purity I demand of you and [priests], and especially of them, in this sacrament. (D2 237)

[GOD:] You would judge that he whose candle weighs an ounce has less of the light than he whose candle weighs a pound. Now the same thing happens to those who receive this Sacrament. Each one carries his own candle, that is the holy desire, with which he receives this Sacrament . . . and lights it by receiving this Sacrament. (D1 231)

[God:] [Come] with love to receive this Sweet and Glorious Light, which I have given you as Food for your service through My ministers, and you receive this Light according to the love and fiery desire with which you approach It. (D1 232)

[God:] You personally participate in this light, that is in the grace which you receive in this Sacrament, according to the holy desire with which you dispose yourselves to receive it. (D1 233)

[God:] My providence has given you food to strengthen you while you are pilgrim travelers in this life. . . . The road is cemented with the blood of my Truth so that you may reach the end for which I created you. (D2 279)

[God:] Do you know the condition of the soul who receives unworthily? She is like a candle on which water has fallen, which can do nothing but crackle when brought near the flame. (D1 233)

[God:] Gaze into the abyss of My love, for there is no rational creature whose heart would not melt for love in contemplating and considering, among the other benefits she receives from Me, the special Gift that she receives in the Sacrament. (D1 234–35)

[God:] The sweet Light of this Sacrament cannot be defiled, divided, or diminished in any way. (D1 234)

[God:] How is this sacrament tasted? With holy desire. The body tastes only the flavor of bread, but the soul tastes me, God and human. So you see, the body's senses can be deceived, but not the soul's. (D2 211)

[God:] Grace lives in such a soul because, having received this bread of life in grace, she lives in grace. (D2 211)

[God:] The perceptions of the body are deluded, but not those of the soul, for she is illuminated and assured in her own perceptions, for she touches with the hand of love that which the eye of her intellect has seen with the pupil of holy faith; and with her palate—that is, with fiery desire—she tastes My Burning Charity, My Ineffable Love, with which I have made her worthy to receive the tremendous mystery of this Sacrament. (D1 237)

[God:] You should receive and look on this Sacrament, not only with bodily perceptions, but rather with your spiritual perceptions ... to receive, and taste, and see this Sacrament. (D1 238)

[God:] I leave you the imprint of grace, as does a seal, which, when lifted from the hot wax upon which it has been impressed, leaves behind its imprint, so the virtue of this Sacrament remains in the soul, that is to say, the heat of My Divine charity and the clemency of the Holy Spirit. There also remains to you the wisdom of My only-begotten Son. (D1 238)

[God:] The Abyss of My loving desire for your salvation has given you, through My dispensation and Divine Providence, coming to the help of your needs, the sweet

Truth as Food in this life, where you are pilgrims and travelers, so that you may have refreshment and not forget the benefit of the Blood. (Di 239)

[C:] Beauty above all beauty; Wisdom above all wisdom—for You are wisdom itself. You, the food of the angels, have given Yourself in a fire of love to men. You, the garment which covers all our nakedness, feed the hungry with Your sweetness. (Di 333)

[C:] Of course you are unworthy. But when do you hope to be worthy? You will be no more worthy at the end than at the beginning. All the good works that we could ever do would never make us worthy, in this sense, of Holy Communion. God alone is worthy of Himself. (V 87)

[C:] Since we need to provision the ship of our soul, let's proceed to provision it there, at that sweetest of channels, the heart and soul and body of Jesus Christ. (L 39)

[C:] We will find that this channel [the body of Christ] flows with so great a love that we will easily be able to fill our souls. So I say to you: don't be slow to put your eye to this open window. (L 39–40)

[C:] The Word has given himself as food, and the Father is a bed where the soul takes its rest. Love! Love! There isn't a thing we lack: a garment of fire against the cold, food against starvation, a bed against exhaustion. (L 235)

CONFESSION

❦

Receive the Holy Spirit. If you forgive the sins of any, they
are forgiven; if you retain the sins of any, they are retained.
—John 20:22–23

[GOD:] It was necessary to leave a continual baptism of
Blood. This the Divine charity provided in the Sacrament of Holy Confession, the soul receiving the Baptism of Blood, with contrition of heart, confessing, when
able, to My ministers who hold the keys of the Blood.
(D1 172–73)

[GOD:] It is true that while you have time you can get
yourselves out of the stench of sin through true repentance and recourse to my ministers. They are the workers who have the keys to the wine cellar, that is, the
blood poured forth from this vine. (D2 62)

[GOD:] Confession is a medicine that heals the effects
of this venom [sin] even while it tastes bitter to selfish
sensuality. (D2 98)

[GOD:] In holy confession, . . . I return to her by grace.
(D2 119)

[GOD:] [Sinners] can confess to my ministers who hold
the key to the blood. This blood the priest pours over
the soul in absolution. (D2 138)

[God:] If they cannot confess, heartfelt contrition is enough for the hand of my mercy to give them the fruit of this precious blood. Still, if they can, I want them to confess. And anyone who could confess but chooses not to will be deprived of the fruit of the blood. (D2 139)

[God:] Let no one be so mad so as to arrange his deeds, that in the hope of receiving it, he puts off confessing until the last extremity of death, when he may not be able to do so. (D1 173)

[God:] You must be firm, you must leave mortal sin by a holy confession, contrition of heart, satisfaction, and purpose of amendment. (D1 287)

[God:] With their tears and sweat [my ministers] anointed the wounds the guilt of deadly sin had made, and those who humbly received this anointing regained perfect health. (D2 229)

[God:] If when they come to the point of death they acknowledge their sin and unload their conscience in holy confession ... what remains is mercy. (D2 267)

[God:] You have to be set free. Leave deadly sin behind by a holy confession with heartfelt contrition, satisfaction, and resolution to sin no more. (D2 331)

[C:] Go to confession often, and seek the company of people who will help you possess God in grace. (L 25)

[C:] First of all, arrange for holy confession, and unburden your consciences. (L 36)

[C:] God's goodness provides for our plight. . . . This is why he has supplied a remedy in holy confession, which derives all its power from the blood of the Lamb. And he gives us this remedy not once or twice, but over and over. (L 135)

[C:] Just as the body cannot survive without food, so the soul cannot survive without God's word and without confession. Guard yourselves against evil companions, for they would be a great obstacle to your holy resolve. (L 213–14)

THE CHURCH

So I now say to you: You are Peter and on this rock I will build my Church. And the gates of the underworld can never hold out against it.—Matthew 16:18

[God:] Take your tears and your sweat, drawn from the fountain of My divine love, and with them wash the face of My spouse. I promise you, that, by this means, her beauty will be restored to her. (D1 73)

[God:] Not by the sword or by war or by violence will she regain her beauty, but through peace and through the constant and humble prayers and sweat and tears poured out by my servants with eager desire. (D2 54)

[God:] All of you together make up one common vineyard, the whole Christian assembly, and you are all united in the vineyard of the mystic body of holy Church from which you draw your life. (D2 62)

[God:] This way of His doctrine, . . . confirmed by the Apostles, declared by the blood of the martyrs, illuminated by the light of the doctors, confessed by the confessors, and narrated in all its love by the Evangelists, all of whom stand as witnesses to confess the Truth, is found in the mystical body of Holy Church. (D1 86–87)

[GOD:] The Apostles, Martyrs, Confessors, Evangelists, and Holy Doctors [have been] placed like lanterns in the Holy Church. (D1 89)

[GOD:] The more the mystic body of holy Church is filled with troubles now, the more it will abound in delight and consolation. And this shall be its delight: the reform of good holy shepherds who are flowers of glory, who praise and glorify my name. (D2 47)

[GOD:] I have set you as workers in your own and your neighbors' souls and in the mystic body of holy Church. In yourselves you must work at virtue; in your neighbors and in the Church you must work by example and teaching. (D2 159)

[GOD:] The Holy Spirit, who is one thing with Me and with My Son, reproved the world by the mouth of the Apostles, with the doctrine of My Truth. They and all others, who are descended from them, following the truth which they understand through the same means, reprove the world. (D1 100)

[GOD:] In His mystical Body, the holy Church, He is administered to whoever will receive Him. He remains wholly with Me, and yet you have Him, whole God and whole man, as . . . in the metaphor of light . . . , if all the world came to take light from it, each would have it entire, and yet it would remain whole. (D1 234)

[GOD:] Sin cannot injure the sacraments of holy Church or lessen their power. But grace is lessened and sin increased in those who administer or receive them unworthily. (D2 215)

[GOD:] I set before you the mystic body of holy Church under the image of a wine cellar. In this wine cellar was the blood of my only-begotten Son, and from this blood all the sacraments derive their life-giving power. (D2 215)

[GOD:] If you turn to Augustine, to the glorious Thomas, to Jerome and the others, you will see what great light they have shed on this bride, as lamps set on a lamp-stand, dispelling errors with their true and perfect humility. (D2 222)

[GOD:] My spouse [is] the Holy Church. (D1 273)

[GOD:] [Holy religion] has been founded by the Holy Spirit [and] appointed as the ship to receive souls who wish to hasten to perfection, and to bring them to the port of salvation. The Captain of this ship is the Holy Spirit. (D1 294–95)

[GOD:] [Religious life] is rich, so that there is no need for the subject to think about his necessities either temporal or spiritual, for if he is truly obedient and observes his order, he will be provided for by his Master, who is the Holy Spirit. (D1 296)

[GOD:] In the days when the religious orders lived virtuously, blossoming with true poverty and fraternal charity, their temporal substance never failed them, but they had more than their needs demanded. (D1 296)

[G<small>OD</small>:] [They] have been washed in the blood, have nursed and been nourished with this blood at the breast of holy Church. (D2 219)

[G<small>OD</small>:] My Church ... is a place of prayer. (D2 248)

[G<small>OD</small>:] See the riches of these holy rules, so thoughtfully and luminously appointed by those who were temples of the Holy Spirit. See with what judgment Benedict ordered his ship; see with what perfection and order of poverty Francis ordered his ship, decked with the pearls of virtue. (D1 296–97)

[G<small>OD</small>:] The gardens of religious life are holy: There are saints in them because they were created and founded in the Holy Spirit. (D2 242)

[G<small>OD</small>:] Look at the ship of your father Dominic, My beloved son: he ordered it most perfectly, wishing that his sons should apply themselves only to My honor and the salvation of souls, with the light of science, which light he laid as his principle foundation. (D1 298)

[G<small>OD</small>:] Look at My glorious Thomas [Aquinas], who gazed with the gentle eye of his intellect at My Truth, whereby he acquired supernatural light and science infused by grace, for he obtained it rather by means of prayer than by human study. He was a brilliant light, illuminating his order and the mystical body of the Holy Church, dissipating the clouds of heresy. (D1 300)

[God:] How displeased I am with the sin of those who persecute holy Church, what disrespect they show for the blood. (D2 272)

[God:] Be humbly attentive to my honor, the salvation of souls, and the reform of holy Church. This will be a sign to me that you and the others love me in truth. (D2 272)

[God:] I repeat My promise, that through the long endurance of My servants I will reform My spouse. Wherefore I invite you to endure, Myself lamenting with you over her iniquities. (D1 327–28)

[C:] I pray and implore you on the part of the Crucified to succour the Spouse in her need, in goods, in persons and in counsel; in every way you possibly can, show that you are a faithful daughter of holy Church. (C 80)

[C:] Be a strong pillar in the garden of Holy Church. (C 144)

[C:] How can you say to me that if you hurt a body, you do not hurt the blood that is in that body? Do you not know that the Church holds in itself the Blood of Christ? (C 94)

[C:] Fortify yourself with the prayers and company of the just. I would like to see them by your side, so that they may be your refreshment in the trials of this life. Besides divine aid, seek to have the help of His servants. (C 168)

[C:] How cruel it is that we who are Christians, members bound together in the body of holy Church, should be persecuting one another! This must not be. (L 80–81)

[C:] In whatever way you can, show yourself a faithful daughter of sweet holy Church. For you know that she is a mother who feeds her children at her breast with sweetest life-giving milk. . . . Be a loyal daughter, always ready to help your mother. (L 102)

[C:] The garden of most holy Church . . . is where all faithful Christians feed, since there is planted the tree of the cross with its burden, the fruit of the Lamb slain for us with such blazing love that it should set every heart afire. (L 168)

[C:] As faithful Christians we ought to be lovers of this holy Church, members bound together in this bride, a mystic body. (L 169)

[C:] I beg you, for love of Christ crucified, to come to the aid of this bride washed in the blood of the Lamb. You see how everyone is harassing her—Christians as well as unbelievers. And you know that one should show one's love when it is needed. (L 169)

[C:] Be strong and steadfastly obedient to holy Church.
(L 243)

[C:] The Church is in need, and so are you. The Church needs your human aid; you need her divine help. Know that the more help you give her, the more you will share in divine grace, the fire of the Holy Spirit that this bride holds within herself. (L 169)

[C:] He took our holy mother Church as his bride. Within her he placed the fruit, the warmth of his blood as a medicine for our sicknesses. I mean the sacraments of the Church, which have received their life in the Blood of God's only-begotten Son. (L 241)

[C:] In the fire of his charity he has so firmly grounded this bride in himself that neither the devil nor anyone else can rob her of her existence. . . . This dear venerable bride will endure forever. (L 241)

[C:] You know well that God is the one who is strong, and all strength and power come from him. This strength has not been taken away from his bride, nor has she been despoiled of this strong steadfast help. (L 241)

[C:] I wish (although not worthy) to shed my blood and give my life and distil the very marrow of my bones for Holy Church. (C 149)

[C:] If all the world should drive me away, I will not care, for I shall find rest, with weeping and with much enduring, on the breast of that sweet Spouse. (C 128)

[C:] Every day You give Yourself to man, representing Yourself in the Sacrament of the Altar, in the body of Your Holy Church. What has done this? Your Mercy. (D1 91)

The Papacy

❧

I will give you the keys of the kingdom of heaven: whatever
you bind on earth shall be considered bound in heaven;
whatever you loose on earth shall be considered loosed in heaven.
—Matthew 16:19–20

[God:] Consider . . . the gentle Gregory, Sylvester, and the other successors of the chief pontiff Peter, to whom my Truth gave the keys of the heavenly kingdom when he said, "Peter, I am giving you the keys of the heavenly kingdom; whatever you loose on earth shall be loosed in heaven, and whatever you bind on earth shall be bound in heaven." (D2 214)

[God:] To whom did [my Son] leave the keys to this blood? To the glorious apostle Peter and to all the others who have come or will come from now until the final judgment day with the very same authority that Peter had. (D2 214–15)

[God:] Christ on earth, then, has the keys to the blood. (D2 215)

[God:] When He returned to Me, rising to Heaven from the conversation of men at the Ascension, He left you this sweet key of obedience; for as you know He left His vicar, the Christ on earth, whom you are all obliged to obey until death. (D1 282–83)

[GOD:] Christ on earth stood at the door of this wine cellar. He had been commissioned to administer the blood, and it was his duty to delegate ministers to help him in the service of the entire universal body of Christianity. (D2 215)

[GOD:] Only those accepted and anointed by him were to thus minister. He was the head of the whole clerical order, and he appointed each one to his proper office to administer this glorious blood. (D2 215)

[GOD:] [Obedience] is the key which opens heaven, which key My Son placed in the hands of His vicar. This vicar placed it in the hands of every one who receives holy baptism, promising therein to renounce the world and all its pomps and delights, and to obey. (D1 286)

[GOD:] The food of the Body and Blood of My Son, wholly God and wholly man [is] administered to you by the hand of My vicar, who holds the key of the Blood. (D1 160)

[GOD:] Peter, the prince of the Apostles ... received the keys of the kingdom of Heaven. (D1 241–42)

[C:] He has the power and the authority and there is no-one who can take it out of his hands, because it was given to him by the first sweet Truth. (C 69)

[C:] Can we dare despise the Blood of Christ? ... He who despises this sweet Vicar, despises the Blood, because he who strikes one, strikes the other, since they are bound together. (C 94)

[C:] Now I shall see if you are truly in love with the reformation of Holy Church; because if you are so in truth, you will follow the will of God and of His vicar. (C 170)

[C:] [Resign yourself] nevertheless to the Pope's will, like one truly obedient. This would be more pleasing to God and more profitable to [yourself]. (C 175)

[C:] [The] soul seems to be dead, because it is separated from the body of the Church. It is not Pope Urban VI you are persecuting, but the truth and our faith. (C 182)

[C:] For the love of God ... affirm it cordially holding that our father is Pope Urban VI, whatever may be said to the contrary. You must obey him and help him and, if necessary, die for this truth. (C 183–84)

[C:] Oh gentle Word, Son of God, you have deposited that blood within the body of holy Church, and you want it to be administered by the hands of your vicar. God's goodness provides for our plight. (L 134–35)

[C:] We would be foolish to break away from this vicar or to act against the one who holds the keys to the blood of Christ crucified. . . . I must not defy him but always humble myself and ask for the blood for mercy's sake. (L 135)

[C:] There is no other way you can have or share in the fruit of the blood. I beg you, for love of Christ crucified, never again rebel against your head. (L 135)

[C:] I would have us humbly rest our heads on the lap of Christ in heaven by our affection and love, and on the lap of Christ on earth (his deputy) by our reverence for the blood of Christ, to which he holds the keys. (L 136)

[C:] Do not wait for time; it is dangerous. Come and hide in the ark of Holy Church under the wings of your father, Pope Urban VI, who holds the keys of the Blood of Christ. (C 184)

[C:] To whomever [the Pope] opens, it is opened; to whom he closes, it is closed. Power and authority are his, and no one can take that power from his hands. It was given him by gentle First Truth. (L 137)

The Priesthood

❧

"As the Father has sent me, even so I send you." And when he had said this, he breathed on them, and said to them, "Receive the Holy Spirit . . ."—John 20:21

[GOD:] [The soul comes] confessing, when able, to My ministers, who hold the keys of the Blood. (D1 173)

[GOD:] They are my workers in the vineyard of your souls, ambassadors for the vineyard of holy Church. (D2 60)

[GOD:] I would satisfy your anguished longings by reforming holy Church through good and holy shepherds. I will do this, as I told you, not through war, not with the sword and violence, but through peace and calm, through my servants' tears and sweat. (D2 159)

[GOD:] I have especially chosen My ministers for the sake of your salvation, so that, through them, the Blood of the humble and immaculate Lamb, My only-begotten Son, may be administered to you. (D1 228)

[GOD:] To [priests] have I given the Sun to administer, giving them the light of [knowledge] and the heat of Divine Love, united together in the color of the Body and Blood of My Son, whose Body is a Sun, because He is one thing with Me, the True Sun. (D1 228–29)

[GOD:] I have dignified my ministers. . . . It is impossible to have a greater dignity than theirs in this life. (D2 212)

[GOD:] They are My anointed ones, and I call them My Christs, because I have given them the office of administering Me to you, and have placed them like fragrant flowers in the mystical body of the holy Church. (D1 240)

[GOD:] To the Holy Spirit is attributed fire and to the Son wisdom, by which wisdom My ministers receive the light of grace, so that they may administer this light to others. (D1 229)

[GOD:] By this means of the Incarnate Word mixed with the Light of My Divine nature and the fiery heat of the Holy Spirit, have you received the Light. Whom have I entrusted with its administration? My ministers in the mystical body of the holy Church, so that you may have life, receiving His Body in food and His Blood in drink. (D1 230)

[GOD:] My ministers ought to be provided by you with material help in their needs, and you ought to be provided for and nourished by them with grace and spiritual gifts, that is, with the holy sacraments I have established in holy Church. (D2 213)

[God:] I want you to know that they give you incomparably more than you give them, for there is no comparison between the finite and passing things with which you help them, and myself, God, who am infinite and have appointed them in my providence and divine charity to minister to you. (D2 213)

[God:] You must not sin against them, because if you do, you are really sinning not against them but against me. (D2 216)

[God:] Recognize the dignity to which I have called My ministers. . . . If they gave their bodies to be burned, they would not repay the tremendous grace and favor which they have received inasmuch as no greater dignity exists in this life. (D1 239–40)

[God:] Your reverence for (My anointed ones) should never fail—not for their own sake, but because of the treasure of the blood. (D2 220)

[God:] The angel himself has no such dignity, for I have given it to those men whom I have chosen for My ministers, and whom I have appointed as earthly angels in this life. (D1 240)

[God:] Even as these ministers require cleanness in the chalice in which this Sacrifice is made, even so do I require the purity and cleanness of their heart and soul and mind. (D1 240)

[GOD:] I have chosen these ministers of mine. They are my anointed ones, stewards of the body and blood of my only-begotten Son—your human flesh joined with my divinity. When they consecrate they stand in the place of Christ my Son. (D2 218)

[GOD:] These gentle ministers of mine, whom I chose and anointed and sent into the mystic body of holy Church ... [give] off within the mystic body of holy Church the brightness of supernatural learning, the color of a holy and honorable life in following the teaching of my Truth, and the warmth of blazing charity. Thus with their warmth they cause barren souls to bring forth fruit. (D2 222)

[GOD:] Those who have been or would be my gentle ministers ... have no use for the world's honors and ranks and pleasures. Therefore, they are not afraid to correct. (D2 225)

[GOD:] In the life eternal I have placed them in the greatest dignity, and they receive blessing and glory in My sight, because they gave the example of an honorable and holy life, and with light administered the Light of the Body and Blood of My only-begotten Son, and all the Sacraments. (D1 252)

[GOD:] You should hold them out to me with tears and great desire, so that I in my goodness may clothe them with the garment of charity. (D2 230)

[G<small>OD</small>:] These My anointed ones and ministers are pecu-
liarly beloved by Me, on account of the dignity which I
placed in them, and because [of] this Treasure which I
placed in their hands. (D1 252–53)

[G<small>OD</small>:] I have given them to you to be your guardians,
to protect you and breathe good inspirations into your
hearts by means of their holy prayers, their teaching, and
the mirror of their lives. (D2 229)

[G<small>OD</small>:] Everyone who is virtuous is worthy of love;
how much more so these, because of the ministry I
have entrusted to them! So because of their virtue and
because of their sacramental dignity you ought to love
them. (D2 230)

[G<small>OD</small>:] In what great reverence you should hold [priests],
for they are My beloved children and shine each as a sun
in the mystical body of the holy Church by their virtues, for every virtuous man is worthy of love, and these
all the more by reason of the ministry which I have placed
in their hands. (D1 256)

[G<small>OD</small>:] These whom I have anointed I have freed from
the world's service and appointed them to serve me alone,
God eternal, by being stewards of the sacraments of holy
Church. (D2 235)

[G<small>OD</small>:] Your pleasures ought to be with the poor and
in visiting the sick, assisting them in their spiritual and

material needs. For no other reason have I made you my minister and given you such dignity. (D2 248)

[GOD:] You know well that if a filthy and badly dressed person brought you a great treasure from which you obtained life, you would not hate the bearer, however ragged and filthy he might be, through love of the treasure and of the lord who sent it to you. . . . You would be anxious through love of his master that he should be cleansed from his foulness and properly clothed. . . . Thus I wish you to act with regard to such badly ordered priests.
  (D1 256–57)

[GOD:] These anointed ones of mine, who ought to be living as angels, should leave dead things to the dead and concern themselves with governing souls. (D2 251)

[GOD:] [Priests] bring you great Treasures—that is to say, the Sacraments of the holy Church—from which you obtain the life of grace, receiving Them worthily . . . through love of Me, the Eternal God, who send them to you. (D1 257)

[GOD:] Their houses ought to be gathering places for my servants and the poor. The bride they hold ought to be the breviary, and the books of Holy Scripture their children. (D2 261)

[GOD:] I want you to know better the treasure of spiritually motivated voluntary poverty. Who knows it? My beloved poor servants. (D2 318)

[C:] Consider your dignity, since God has in mercy given you the great distinction of having to dispense the fire of divine charity, the body and blood of Christ crucified. Just think! Not even the angels have such dignity!

(L 277)

[C:] See how God has put his word into the vessel of your soul. You know very well that when you speak in the person of Christ, you have the authority to consecrate that wonderful sacrament. (L 277)

Marriage and Family Life

❦

Every sound tree bears good fruit, but the bad tree bears evil fruit.—Matthew 7:17

[C:] I don't want you to forget about making amends for your ingratitude and inattentiveness; you owe this to your mother, to whom you are obligated by God's commandment. (L 32)

[C:] It is you who are obligated to [your mother], not she to you. She didn't take *your* flesh, but gave you hers. (L 33)

[C:] Remember to go to confession, you and your family as well. (L 33)

[C:] You will hear at the end those sweet words: "Come, my blessed son, and possess the kingdom of heaven, because you conscientiously cast aside desire and affection for conformity to the world, and reared and nurtured your family in holy fear of me. Now I am giving you perfect rest." (L 117)

[C:] I beg you to rear and nurture your children in the fear of God. Be concerned not only for their physical needs but for the good of their souls as well. Know that on the last day God will demand an account of them from you. (L 210)

[C:] With desire have I desired, my dear son, to see you so bound and united in virtue with your family, and especially with your wife, that neither the devil nor anyone else can break that bond or release you from it. (L 221)

[C:] I long to see you a real father, nurturing, ruling, and governing your family in such fear of God that you will be a fruitful tree, and that the fruit you have borne will be good and virtuous. (L 299)

[C:] Be a real father in nurturing your soul and the children God has given you, growing constantly from virtue to virtue. (L 301)

[C:] You will not tolerate your children and your family offending him either, but will correct them as a true father. As far as it is within your control, you will want them to follow in his footsteps. Now I beg you to be conscientious about this. (L 301)

[C:] Encourage and bless the whole family. . . . Keep living in God's holy and tender love. (L 301)

[C:] They are led and bound more by gentleness than by other force or by harsh words. (C 188)

[C:] Children should be loved for the love of Him who created them, and not for the love of self nor of the children. (V 104)

The Mass

❦

A man once gave a great banquet.
—Luke 14:16

[God:] [At the altar you paused to] consider My love, which had made you worthy to hear Mass. (D1 236)

[God:] With humility [the prelates] trampled pride underfoot and like angels approached the table of the altar. (D2 223)

[God:] They celebrated [the Mass] with bodily purity and spiritual sincerity, set ablaze as they were in charity's furnace. (D2 223)

[God:] [Wait] with great longing to be able to receive communion. (D2 295)

[God:] Do you not see what great grace you have received simply to be in the holy temple of God? (D2 296)

[God:] [The soul] prepares the table of the most holy cross in her heart and spirit. When it is set, she finds there the food of the gentle loving Word—the sign of my honor and your salvation, for which my only-begotten Son's body was opened up to give you himself as food. (D2 177)

[GOD:] I created your soul with a capacity for loving—so much so that you cannot live without love. Indeed, love is your food. . . . It is with this love that you come to receive my gracious glorious light, the light I have given you as food, to be administered to you by my ministers. (D2 208)

[GOD:] My deep charity gave him to you as food for your salvation and for your nourishment in this life where you are pilgrim travelers. . . . I in my divine providence gave you this food, my gentle Truth, to help you in your need. (D2 212)

[GOD:] It is the body and blood of Christ crucified, wholly God, wholly human, the food of angels and the food of life. It is a food that satisfies the hungry soul who finds joy in this bread, . . . for it is a food that must be taken with the mouth of holy desire and tasted in love. (D2 279)

[C:] [God] feeds us at the table of the Lamb, who is there as our food and our waiter. For you see, the Father is for us a table bearing everything. (L 189)

[C:] I long to see you in your place at the table of the most holy cross. There we find the spotless Lamb, who has been made food and table and waiter for us. . . . No other food can please or satisfy the soul. (L 312)

BAPTISM

The water I shall give will turn into a spring inside him, welling up to eternal life.—John 4:14

[GOD:] In my unspeakable love for you I willed to create you anew in grace. So I washed you and made you a new creation in the blood that my only-begotten Son poured out with such burning love. (D2 29)

[GOD:] It was by virtue of the blood that they were freed in holy baptism from the taint of original sin, which they had contracted when they were conceived by their father and mother. (D2 51)

[GOD:] Holy Baptism . . . has the virtue of communicating the life of grace by means of that glorious and precious Blood. (D1 69)

[GOD:] At the moment that the soul receives Holy Baptism, original sin is taken away from her, and grace is infused into her. (D1 69)

[GOD:] Manfully, then, should you follow this road, without any cloud of doubt, but with the light of faith that has been given you as a principle in Holy Baptism. (D1 88)

[GOD:] But why did he say, "I am the fountain of living water"? Because when the divine nature was joined with the human nature, he became the fountain holding me, the source of living water. (D2 106)

[GOD:] In order to give them eternal life, I created them in My image and likeness and re-created them to grace with the Blood of My Son, making them sons of adoption. (D1 144)

[GOD:] I wished you to see the secret of the Heart, showing it to you open, so that you might see how much more I loved than I could show you by finite pain. I poured from it Blood and Water, to show you the baptism of water, which is received in virtue of the Blood.
(D1 172)

[GOD:] Though My works, that is the pains of the Cross, were finite, the fruit of them which you receive in Baptism, through Me, are infinite. This is in virtue of the infinite Divine nature, united with the finite human nature. (D1 173)

[GOD:] He, by stripping himself of life, clothed you anew in innocence and grace. You receive this innocence and grace in holy baptism by the power of the blood that washes away the stain of original sin in which you were conceived. (D2 279)

[GOD:] Without the light, no one can walk in the truth, that is, without the light of reason. [This] light of reason you draw from Me the True Light, by means of the eye of your intellect and the light of faith which I have given you in holy baptism. (D1 207)

[GOD:] In baptism, and through the mediation of the Blood of My only-begotten Son, you have received the form of faith; which faith you exercise in virtue by the light of reason, which gives you life and causes you to walk in the path of truth, and by its means, to arrive at Me, the True Light. (D1 207)

[GOD:] You would be like a candle with no wick inside it, which cannot burn or receive light, if you have not received in your souls the wick which catches this Divine Flame, that is to say, the Holy Faith, which you receive by grace in baptism. (D1 231–32)

[C:] Can you not see that they were all were created by that most pure rose of the eternal will of God and recreated to grace in that most ardent crimson rose of the Blood of Christ. (C 185–86)

[C:] My soul longs to see you come to the light of holy baptism, just as the deer longs for living water. Put up no more resistance to the Holy Spirit who is calling you. (L 282)

THE BIBLE

Heaven and earth will pass away, but my words will not pass away.—Matthew 24:35

[God:] Holy Scripture ... seemed dark because it was not understood; not through any defect of the Scriptures, but of them who heard them, and did not understand them. Wherefore I sent this light [Thomas Aquinas] to illuminate the blind and coarse understanding, uplifting the eye of the intellect to know the Truth. (D1 182)

[God:] They are not afraid of the devil's delusions; because of the supernatural light of grace and the light of Holy Scripture, they recognize them for what they are and they suffer neither darkness nor spiritual distress from them. (D2 266)

[God:] Everything he said was said especially to the disciples but in a more general way to everyone then and to all those who would come in the future. (D2 119)

[God:] The light [is] given by grace, given to whoever wants to receive this light beyond natural light. Every light that comes from Holy Scripture has come and still comes from that light. (D2 157)

[GOD:] Foolish, proud, and learned people ... read Scripture literally rather than with understanding. They taste only its letter ... never tasting the marrow of Scripture because they have let go of the light by which Scripture was formed and proclaimed . (D2 157)

[GOD:] Holy Scripture is lightsome in itself, and my chosen ones drew from it with a supernatural light from me the true light. (D2 239)

[GOD:] He taught you not only with words but by his example as well, from his birth right up to the end of his life. (D2 320)

The Saints

❦

The virtuous will shine like the sun in the kingdom of their Father.— Matthew 13:43

[GOD:] The desire of the blessed is to see My honor in you wayfarers who are pilgrims. . . . In their desire for My honor, they desire your salvation, and always pray to Me for you. (D1 112)

[GOD:] [My saints] made themselves small for me, and I have made them great in myself, everlasting Life, and in the mystic body of holy Church. For they are forever remembered because their names are written in me, the book of life. (D2 142)

[GOD:] The saints enjoy mutual charity, and they also love you who are pilgrim travelers in this world, put here by me to reach your final goal in me, eternal Life. (D2 176)

[GOD:] [The martyrs'] death was life-giving. They raised the dead and drove out the darkness of deadly sin. The world with all its grandeur, with all its lords and their power, could not defend itself against them. . . . This virtue stands like a lamp set on a lampstand. (D2 178–79)

[GOD:] The blessed come from their weeping to gladness. They receive everlasting life with the fruit of their tears and flaming charity; they cry out and offer tears of fire for you in my presence. (D2 182)

[GOD:] In everlasting life they have not lost that love; no, they still love and share with each other even more closely and fully, adding their love to the good of all. (D2 83)

[GOD:] See generosity and mercy [will be] shining in the blessed ones, who receive the fruit of the Blood of the Lamb. The pains that they have borne remaining as ornaments on their bodies, like the dye upon the cloth, not by virtue of the body but only out of the fullness of the soul. (D1 116)

[GOD:] The good of these souls is beyond what your mind's eye can see or your ear hear or your tongue describe or your heart imagine. What joy they have in seeing me who am all good! (D2 84)

[GOD:] You see, then, how the saints and all souls who have eternal life are desirous of the salvation of souls, but without pain. Their death put an end to their pain, but not to their loving charity. (D2 152)

[GOD:] All of [the saints] are living witnesses to the truth in the mystic body of holy Church. They are like lamps set on a lampstand to point out the way of truth, perfectly lighted, that leads to life. (D2 69)

[G**OD**:] [The saints] pass through the Narrow Gate, bathed in the Blood of Christ crucified, and they find themselves in Me, the Sea Pacific, raised from imperfection . . . and arrived at perfection, satisfied by every good. (D1 178)

[G**OD**:] I have shown the ignorant where to find those who point out and teach this way that is truth. These are, I said, the apostles and evangelists, the martyrs and confessors and holy doctors, who have been set like lamps in holy Church. (D2 70–71)

[G**OD**:] They are like precious stones, and as such do they stand in My presence, because I have received their labor and poverty and the light which they shed with the odor of virtues in the mystic body of the holy Church. (D1 252)

[G**OD**:] After the prophets I provided for you in the coming of the Word, who was your mediator with me, God eternal. And after him I sent the apostles, the martyrs, the doctors and confessors. All these things my providence has done, and so, I tell you, will I continue to provide for you right up to the end. (D2 282)

[G**OD**:] What has placed them in so blessed a state? The blood of the Lamb. (D1 291)

[G**OD**:] With this light that is given to the eye of the intellect, Thomas Aquinas saw Me, wherefore he acquired the light of much science; also Augustine, Jerome, and the doctors, and My saints. They were illuminated by My Truth to know and understand My Truth [Holy Scripture]. (D1 182)

[C:] Your mercy is life-giving. It is the light in which both the upright and sinners discover your goodness. Your mercy shines forth in your saints in the height of heaven. And if I turn to the earth, your mercy is everywhere. (D2 72)

[C:] Keep on the battlefield with the standard of the most holy Cross; think that the blood of our glorious martyrs is always crying out in the sight of God, invoking His help upon you. (C 180)

[C:] The bodies of those glorious martyrs are buried here in Rome; but their blood, which they shed with such fire of love in giving their lives for Life, their blood boils up, inviting you and the others to come and endure for the glory of God and Holy Church. (C 171)

[C:] Oh Jesus, gentlest love, let your will be done in us always as it is in heaven by your angels and saints! (L 201)

[C:] Respond to the call and loving mercy of the Holy Spirit who summons you so gently, who makes God's servants raise their voices in your behalf before him that you may be granted the life of grace. (L 138)

[C:] In conversing with the Just, the soul neither can nor will rejoice in their joy, but only in the hunger they still have, and used to have while they were pilgrims and wayfarers in this life. (C 195)